❧ANCHOR AND HOPE❧

ANCHOR ❧ AND ❧ HOPE

Jo Anderson

HODDER AND STOUGHTON
LONDON   SYDNEY   AUCKLAND   TORONTO

Endpaper: The Pool in 1888 by Vicat Cole: Thames sailing barge and lighters, left; steam tug, right centre; stackies and canal barge, right.

Facing the title page: Barge roads, below bridge in the 'twenties.

British Library Cataloguing in Publication Data
Anderson, Jo
  Anchor and hope.
  1. London metropolitan area – Social life
  and customs
  1. Title
  942.1   DA688

ISBN 0 340 23071 1

DEDICATED TO A LARGE FAMILY

I do not know much about Gods; but I think that the river
Is a strong brown god – sullen, untamed, and intractable,
Patient to some degree, at first recognised as a frontier;
Useful, untrustworthy, as a conveyor of commerce;
Then only a problem confronting the builder of bridges.
The problem once solved, the brown god is almost forgotten
By dwellers in cities – ever, however, implacable,
Keeping his seasons and rages, destroyer, reminder
Of what men choose to forget.

T. S. Eliot, *Four Quartets*

❧ACKNOWLEDGMENTS❧

THE COMPLETION OF this book would not have been possible without the generous help of many riversiders and concerned organisations. I would like to thank the Leverhulme Trust for granting me a Research Award which made it possible to visit and interview some fascinating people, and Julian Watson of the Greenwich Local History Museum, and Miss Boast of the Newington District Library, Southwark, for their help and encouragement on several rainy days in 1977. I am also indebted to the Society for Spritsail Barge Research, Mr. Harris of Crescent Shipping (Rochester) Ltd., Roger Norman of the *South East London and Kentish Mercury*, and Christopher Cove Smith of the Inland Waterways Association, for putting me in touch with members. Mr. A. Steatham of Eltham, Percy W. Mitchell of Bromley and Captain Les Williams of Sittingbourne for their written reminiscences which they sent to me. But above all, the following riversiders who helped so much to recall a world almost past: Capt. Vic Wadhams of Rochester, Bob Harris (for permission to quote from Harry Thomas Harris's notebooks), Capt. Charlie Jackson of Charlton, Capt. and Mrs. Bertie Fry of Greenhithe, Capt. Dick Virgo and Mr. S. E. Godwin of Strood, Capt. B. J. Farthing of Rochester, Mrs. Nellie Shackel of Battersea, Mr. Bob Sargent of Charlton, Mr. C. Anderson of Bean, Kent, and Mr. S. Watson of Kilmington, Devon (for use of family photographs). Sincere thanks also to Don Abel of the tug *Cemenco* for 'taking me in tow' down the Thames in 1978, and Alan Lee Williams, O.B.E., M.P., Tom Sadler and Jack Faram of T.O.W. at the Royal Albert Docks. The quotation from T. S. Eliot's 'The Dry Salvages' is reproduced from his *Four Quartets* by permission of Faber and Faber Limited.

*London Dock
bogey man, 1890's.*

Licensed Riverside porter late 19th century.

TSB mate 1870's in canvas smock and soft gallies.

CONTENTS

1   The Day of the Red Herring   13
2   Beginnings   22
3   Muck and Brass   36
4   The Hulks   45
5   Sail and Steam   53
6   The Chain Gang   67
7   Mudlarks   77
8   The Old Gel   83
9   Thames Traffic   96
10 In Living Memory   110
11 Friends and Neighbours   131
12 Dead 'Uns and Downalong   147
13 High Days and Holidays   162
14 Some Particularly Favourite Target   172
15 The Turning Tide   183

Appendix – The Bread Basket Department   195
Bibliography   205

ANCHOR AND HOPE

❦ I ❦

The Day of the Red Herring

The smell of Sunday morning
God gave to us as ours . . .
                    G. K. Chesterton

THE FIRST GLIMMERINGS that my family roots were unusual dawned one ear-burning day when I was twelve years old. The fateful question in the never-to-be-forgotten English class was insignificant enough on the face of it. 'Miss', the teacher, she of the piercing eye and voice that could peel paint off the walls, placed a long finger upon my right shoulder and asked me to explain to the class the meaning of the phrase 'a red herring'. My face glowed with pleasure, for here was a question I could answer at length. I stood up confidently. "A red herring," I explained, looking at all the bobs and pigtails, "is a silver fish about ten inches long. It should be stiff and firm, with shiny eyes, and it's caught off the Thames estuary. We catch them off Yantlet Creek," I added unnecessarily, because I could see I was losing them. "When you catch it, you steep it in red vinegar." I began to catch the unmistakable sounds of muffled giggles. "You put some cloves in – you take all the bones out of course – and you always eat it on Sundays at four p.m. . . . or we do at Grandad's . . ." I continued rather lamely, because by this time the class was in uproar. Miss's arm assumed the upraised horizontal which signified 'Go-to-the-front-of-the-class-and-stand-there-with-your-hands-on-your-head-you-silly-girl', and I slunk off feeling as daft as a brush amidst scornful sniggers.

[13]

Years later, despite memories of many subsequent ear-burning gaffs, nothing has ever quite superseded the sense of injustice and humiliation felt that day, for, surely, a 'red herring', apart from its metaphorical use, *was* a semi-raw fish, boned and steeped in red vinegar, which was eaten with relish on the best plates on the best tablecloth, at Grandad's little house in Charlton whenever we went there, to sit amongst the ticking clocks and burnished barometers in which you could see your face, of a Sunday afternoon at four p.m.

Those Sundays were ritual family gatherings, when corporate decisions were made, and the world in general discussed. My father, his three brothers and two sisters with assorted wives and offspring, would sit quietly and respectfully listening to the gruff but warm voice of this cragged old patriarch in his best navy-blue suit. Grandad's hands were like two bunches of pork sausages. They had fascinating tattoos etched across their backs. His hands could crack a walnut in a single effortless clench, or weave the most delicate lace-like patterns with a piece of string. I would often catch him fingering a piece of twine and forming it into intricate knots and plaits as he pondered a question, rather like others might finger a rosary. He was a man who never made a hasty utterance but always emitted an aura of quiet authority and experience; a man who could silence a son at a glance with eyes that were bright with humour.

On slow walks at his side, I noticed that he could name the line, tonnage, and cargo of a ship from a quick glance at its funnel as it broke through the mists several miles out in the Thames estuary – and occasionally he would chuckle under his breath as he saw some ghost of the past on the grey water fifty years away from the ugly oil-tankers that I saw spilling their muck across the beaches. He always ate red herrings on Sundays at four p.m., and not knowing it at that time, because I was so lost in my own all-consuming humiliation, I had illustrated a weekly ritual inherent amongst a group of people who had lived beside the river Thames and worked on its waters all their lives.

Grandad had been a sailorman – a sailing barge skipper, one of a proud artisan class of watermen who had been part of the life's blood of London through the centuries.

My dad, and his brothers and sisters had grown up in the labyrinth of small streets that lined the wharves and tiers of Charlton, where the bowsprits of ships hovered over the ends of the streets, and a forest of funnels and masts had jostled for berths in the then thriving docklands

Grandad with his 'peepers' at Yantlet Creek.

opposite. They had carried with them into the green quiet of Kent memories of when West Street and Heringham Road, on Charlton riverside had been a cacophony of porters' barrows, ear-splitting rending of old timbers as the sailing ships were broken up in the Outer Basin, and the local pubs loud with the accents of Dutchmen, barge-men, lighermen and ferrymen arguing over the next sail-race in the Anchor & Hope, and the Waterman's Arms.

I was the apple of Grandad's eye, being the second youngest cousin then, and in those odd Sundays, and on annual camping holidays on the Kent marshes, he had endeavoured to transmit to me (no doubt lamenting the fact that I wasn't a boy) a love of the sea and ships, and memories of a fascinating riverside community: a com-munity which, along with their streets, and two-up-two-downers as well as their magnificently graceful red-sailed barges, has almost passed into extinction as a working force.

Grandad, like most independent men of his day, wanted the best for his four sons and two daughters – and the best meant something better than the back-breaking insecurity of barging, when the writing was already on the wall, and he was having to augment a meagre livelihood by working the cable-ships. The best meant nightschool at the local Poly – an apprenticeship and a trade in the mechanical world which had such a stranglehold on his beloved sail, and thus all his sons became skilled men and gradually drifted away from the waterside, coming together again after the Second World War and the Navy, with a brood of toddlers for the formal Sunday tea in the small council house in Charlton where Grandad had been rehoused. As the afternoon progressed into dusk, talk from the parlour would become more animated, punctuated by roars of laughter, as somebody recalled 'Old Mother No Nose' or some other long-gone waterfront neighbour. The giggles would be interspersed with Grandad's customary 'Cor stone-a-crows!' as he fingered his 'roll-yer-own' cigarette with its evil tobacco, or weaved another piece of string as he pondered one of the innumerable characters who had adorned that colourful neighbourhood.

Only one uncle, Ted, remained on the docks, driving a heavy tanker for Tate & Lyle. Now he, too, has moved out with his family to Norfolk, a significant choice really, for in East Anglia lie similar flat open marshlands, sandbanks and dykes to those which at one time interspersed the little houses in Charlton and Greenwich. In a sense, he has returned to his roots. My father and mother eventually moved to Axmouth – a small village in Devon on the wide, straddling banks of the Axe where it runs into the sea, and this too, was a return to childhood – geographically many miles away, but containing the same inherited opportunities for fishing, beach-combing and just plain staring at the eddies and moving tides. For whilst being a geographical part of London life, along with the attendant waterpeople who were his neighbours, the humpers, lightermen, hufflers, pilots, fishermen, sailmakers, shipwrights, ferrymen, and coastal sailors, the bargeman was essentially a man of the open spaces. He was neither a townsman, countryman, nor seaman, but a mixture of all three, which can be discerned still in the oddly difficult to catch dialect, which is dying with them. His real element was the wide open marsh of Kent and Essex with its curlews, and crabs, shellfish and mustard-smelling grass and turf. What they didn't know about the marshes wasn't worth knowing, and only Charles Dickens amongst writers, has for me, caught the essence of the marshes.

Recently, I drove down to Allhallows to see our old hunting grounds, and to my great sadness found that successive bands of holidaymakers had uprooted the old crossing places, and the once wild horses and bullocks which roamed there, were now blasé about

Top: *Yantlet Creek today with the Isle of Grain power station on the horizon.*

Below: *Allhallows, its once navigable channels now silted up.*

humans wandering through them. A huge, ugly power station scars the horizon on Grain and has supplanted the great fortress where we youngsters risked life and limb on the huge parapets, 'Beau Geste' one day, 'William the Conk' another. The spit at Yantlet Creek where we fished for herring has fallen into the sea and disappeared into the mud. It all seemed smaller – tamed somehow, and of the thousands of huge mushrooms we used to gather, I found but one small button. The sea-wall was cracked and broken, its concrete slabs invaded by sea-kale and thistles.

[17]

Until Grandad's death in 1962, the whole tribe of us spent each summer camping on those marshes for weeks on end. We camped in ex-W.D. bell-tents, sleeping like spokes round a wheel-hub. The days were spent running about like a bevy of wild young savages under the eye of Grandad up on the sea-wall with his 'peepers' or binoculars. Dad and uncles went off eeling, rabbiting, duck-shooting or fishing in their kayaks, whilst Mum and aunts prepared delicious plates of field mushrooms which had been gathered in the early morning sunshine. Great dinner-plates they were, sliced like cake, and simmering in bacon fat, and glutinous black ink. Some-times we'd go eeling with Grandad, who would creep along the dyke's edge, his three-pronged spear held aloft. Suddenly he'd catch sight of tell-tale air bubbles, and the spear would slash into the mud with unfaltering accuracy, to be pulled out again with a huge, writhing eel on its prongs. Sometimes we'd gather winkles – always on the falling tide, and always off the rocks. We'd wade into the clearer swatchways, snatch up a bucketful of sea-water, and build an open driftwood fire on the shingle. The winkles were always boiled in sea-water, boiling in fresh-water being 'a landsman's habit which boils out all the sea-taste' as Grandad 'larned us', and these would be voraciously attacked at tea-time with bent safetypins and pushed down with doorsteps of bread and butter, whilst the clan sprawled round the fire in the centre of assembled tents.

We'd stride off to small inlets and creeks with emotive names like Egypt Bay, and Mary Bay, not knowing that they were Grandad's old stamping grounds when the Thames was alive with red-sails, mostly on legitimate freight, but occasionally, Grandad would whisper archly 'for a quick snatch of a sheep'. He joked that that was why you got three-legged sheep on the marshes, where some skipper had grabbed the Sunday joint for Mum in 'Happy Valley', which was his, and all homecoming sailormen's name for Charlton long before the football fans coined it for their team. 'Better to hang for a sheep than a lamb', he maintained had originated with those clandestine landfalls.

We travelled like a band of wandering tinkers – we'd pile out of the mainline train at Gravesend, and await the ancient little two-carriage puffer that would take us along the branch line through Chalk, Hoo and Stoke to the end of the line and the start of the marshes. Many times, Grandad would hail another old-timer, dressed in navy-blue like himself, with the same sloping shoulders and gnarled hands, and they'd talk of the past, whilst we impatiently waited for the 'puffer' to haul itself squeaking and protesting from the sidings and transport us to Allhallows-on-mud as it was known. Now the little station is sadly fallen into a wreck, surrounded by a caravan park. The rails have been ripped up, and the neat mahogany waiting room piled high with rusty cans. One more thing lost to time.

Even as a child, it was obvious to me that all those creeks and inlets had seen a bigger population. At Yantlet where the Thames widens to meet the sea there were signs of a village that's now collapsed into the sea. We would find school ink-pots, clay-pipes and hundreds of other indications of an old fishing village and locals would whisper archly of 'Dead Man's Creek' and 'Queen Victoria's meeting place', a once secluded landing stage, now under the soulful eyes of the oil refinery. During the Second World War, the whole marsh area had been traversed by rail-lines running over the dykes, to enable ammunition to be brought to the big coastal guns assembled there. Submarine nets and winches stood rusting on Allhallows beaches, and all around the coast stood stark pillboxes and fortresses. The whole area had a history of smuggling, and it wasn't so far back when two of us found ourselves outside a concrete gun emplacement, right round the headland between Mary Bay and Egypt Bay. We pushed our way in and found ourselves looking at a row of some fifty brand new Japanese motor-bikes, all neatly wrapped up in plastic, and waiting to be spirited to London. The shore there is glutinous marshland, and the nearest road some three miles inland, connected by a thin track. Smuggling, it would seem, is still carried on, though the Customs would be unlikely to shear the owner's barge in half, and press its crew into the Royal Navy as was the custom a hundred years before. That the smuggler was a barge is in no doubt; nothing else could have got so close inshore, nor had the capacity to carry such a load, so some barge skipper somewhere had found a way to survive the motorway and the juggernaut lorry.

All those seemingly unrelated crafts of eeling, reading the tides, and marshes, I took for granted. For I did not realise that those family jaunts were the last vestiges for my family of the bargeman's tradition when an annual holiday meant a snatched weekend under canvas, and the trim-tram net. On those long summer days I learnt much about bargemen indirectly, without knowing it at the time. I learnt to recognise that peculiar shambling, rolling walk, born of years on a deck. I got used to those hands, which fascinated me as a child, sculpted by the wind and frost, ice on the rigging, and fingers split open in a dozen gales. The old bargemen were stamped with such character you could pick them out in a football crowd. Today I still recognise them, old men sitting in the back bar of a waterfront pub at Southwark perhaps, huge hams round a pint, the eyes staring out to some distant horizon. I've gone into the pubs around the Borough Market Bankside, and seen those hunched figures, vaguely sullen until I mention that I'm Ted Anderson's grand-daughter, and then the eyes light up. I get the feeling I'm one of them, albeit once removed, and they nudge me with a chuckle: 'Ah, them's were the days' – 'yer grandad will tell yer . . .' Grandad can't, he died of cancer in 1962. They told him he had the 'killer' and the proud old man simply gave up the ghost with a gruff "I'll not be a burden to anyone". He died when I was eight thousand miles away in Singapore, but remembering back to all those childhood incidents, I knew that he knew I should remember them.

On the occasional walk through Rotherhithe, I look at the empty houses and deserted jetties, except for the odd wharfside pub which has become a chic watering-place. Woolwich has became a waste-land of high-rise flats and over-passes and under-passes. The old Woolwich Ferry with its smelly pistons, thumping up and down through shining brass, as the white-coated engineer caressed the gleaming works with cotton-waste, and the bows soap-sudded into great spumes of bubbles when *John Burns* or *Will Crooks* thudded away across the Thames with us kids leaning excitedly over the rail in Grandad's firm grasp, has been replaced by a concrete monstrosity with all the charm of a floating bedstead. It's all going and with it a life of indescribable hardship when cargoes were not forthcoming and there was not enough in the tin on the mantelpiece to pay the tally-man. The working conditions of the bargemen would negate it in the twentieth century even if the motorway hadn't, for no union on earth would tolerate their way of doing things. But its traditions and its people deserve to be recorded.

In a recent telephone call to a borough archive which shall be nameless, I asked the archivist if she had any photographs of sailing-bargemen and their families, at work or play. Her reply sent me flying back to my 'red herring' day again. "To my knowledge," she said, "bargees just spent all their money in the pubs getting drunk." My grandfather would have bridled at the word, 'bargee' and exploded at the suggestion that he drank his family's livelihood away in a pub, and her misguided remark seemed, even to my scanty recollections, totally unconnected with my memories of the sailor-men and their families I knew as a child.

The time seemed ripe, therefore, to explore their history and beginnings, to trace and listen to those waterfront people I could find, and record their traditions, memories, and struggles. This first chapter is written at the beginning of my journey, and at this stage I have, apart from childhood memories, no more historical know-ledge than the average reader. What I have are disorientated jigsaw pieces, a remembered snatch of conversation perhaps, a dialect word, a few hazy images, an enigmatic look or a phrase which sticks in the mind.

Many fine books have been written of the river-craft themselves, but a ship is a dormant vessel, which comes alive only when she is handled by the crew that knows her. Those crews held a knowledge of wind and tide which take us back in an unbroken line to the days of Drake and Cook, and some of them are still alive, waiting to tell me of their craft. Behind them are staunch and courageous women, the youngest in their seventies now. When they go, skills handed down through generations will go with them, and before all of us whose roots were by the Thames forget that 'red herring' has more than one meaning, perhaps I can turn the pages back a few years and let the waterfront people speak for themselves.

The *Gordon*, *Imperial Woolwich Free Ferry*.

2

Beginnings

The Thames . . . is the privileged place for fish
and ships, the glory and wealth of the city,
the highway to the sea, the bringer in of
wealth and strangers, and his business is
all for water, yet he deals much with the
land too: He is a little sea and a great
river.

Donald Lupton, 1632

THE THAMES HAD once been a tributary of the Rhine, when densely
wooded shores teemed with bison, and our riverside native squatted
by the water fashioning his rough, straight-sided trog in which he
fished, and paddled through a maze of tributaries and marshland.
Through the centuries he was to watch invaders come and go, and
from each he would learn and adapt to suit his own river environ-
ment.

The Romans were quick to realise the potential of a trading settlement with an open route to the sea, and Celtic Llyn-din, stronghold
by the marshes, became their Londinium and grew on the high
ground forty miles upstream. With them the Romans brought their
'bargas', flat-bottomed boats for navigating shallow waters and
carrying goods, and a technique which they had themselves learned
from the ancient Egyptians on the Nile where such a vessel could be
handily manoeuvred downstream by drifting with the current and a
drag anchor. 'Drudging', a technique used by Thames sailing
bargemen for centuries had arrived.

Our riverside ancestor, now earning a comfortable living piloting the bargas through the twisting channels and selling his fish to the imperial garrisons, watched them pass and noted with interest the fine square mainsail of the longboat which made it so manoeuvrable.

The next invaders, the Saxons, unable to attack London successfully, settled themselves around it, and gave us our 'tons' – Brixton, Kennington, Charlton – town of the churls or small farmers who reared pigs along the riverside. The local natives were quick to adopt the Saxon method of netting fish, giving to London tradition the technique of peter-net fishing.

The Vikings, when they arrived, settled themselves on the high ground of Blackheath beyond the fumes of the Saxon's hog stalls, and swept boldly round the bend of the river to attack and pillage. The riversider noted once again the ease with which the Norsemen steered their craft by means of a *stjonbordi,* a paddle worked over the right side of the boat, which he adapted as 'starboard'.

London with its river artery was taking embryo shape, and names still extant on our modern maps point to their beginnings: Southwark – Suthringe weorc, bridgehead on the marshes; Depeford; Merton – meretone, town on the marsh; Rotherhithe – rethrahythe, sailors' haven; Greenwich – Grenevic, green town. Some thirty miles downriver at Geresend (Gravesend), stood a sizeable town where the locals piloted merchant galleys upriver from the point where the Saxon 'portgereve's' authority started, and the Saxon sailors (or 'morgans') intermingled happily with the natives.

Our early English waterman happily intermarried with Saxon and Dane, but had little use for the bridge the Romans had built upriver. On the Kentish side of the Thames, therefore, they spoke the old English of the Jutes, watching the clouds in the 'welkin' and perfecting their 'craft'. While across the water the Essex men had acquired a Scandinavian dialect and admired the clouds in the 'sky' and brushed up their 'skill' with the mackerel net – an idea pinched from visiting Phoenicians. The inhabitant of Londinium swept up the remains left by the Roman and gabbled his rapid Mercian which neither Kentish nor Essex man could understand. By the eleventh century the Dane had been sent packing, and the riversider happily launched his barge with its square sail and ringed brails (also swiped from the Romans), and as the sun set on the invaders, his shallow craft with its single sail presented to the shore a silhouette which was to enhance the River Thames for centuries.

The reason for London's birth, therefore, was the river and

shipping. By the seventeenth century all the inhabitants of the City and its environs, from the heart to the estuary forty miles downriver, drew their livelihoods either directly or indirectly from the river. This was the unifying factor for both rich and poor being there, and never in our history can our roots have been so clear. The Thames was the great maritime trading centre for merchants and their affiliated bodies, fish market, the City's High Street, arena for any spectacle of note, and port all rolled into one.

It is difficult to realise now that all Londoners were once riversiders. For apart from the fact that the Thames flooded at each high tide over a wider area, and is now held back behind artificial embankments, there were dozens of other tributary rivers which were used as thoroughfares much as in Venice today. We have lost the feel for boats and boating which was second nature to the first Elizabethan Londoners before the Thames' tributaries disappeared under tarmac.

Wherever there was a stream the houses clustered. The richer the house, the closer to the water's edge because latrines could be erected over the river. The Westbourne River started out of Hampstead Heath and gushed down to Knightsbridge where the bejewelled merchant had to pay a hefty toll to the riversiders before he could be hoisted on shoulders and carried across the rapids. The Fleet River, now dammed up in Kenwood Park, was until the nineteenth century a dangerous rapid over six hundred feet wide where it flowed into the Thames, and still so prominent in the nineteenth century that Nelson could keep his eye on the Fleet from his bedroom window in Kentish Town three miles away. The speed of the Fleet's current was ideal for the many paper mills which grew up along its banks, and produced fine parchment. Its power was also harnessed for the milling of corn and producing of minerals for gunpowder – all this where Farringdon Street runs now. Oyster smacks once unloaded their catch at Holborn. The Walbrook, which rose near the old Saxon settlement of Islington, flowed down through herds of cows into Moorfields. Where Mansion House stands now were busy wharves specialising in the unloading and storage of corn from Syrian barges, tin and lead from Cornwall, spices and condiments from the Middle East. Hundreds of springs noted for their sweet water bubbled out at Sadler's Wells, Trafalgar Square and Shaftesbury Avenue, and there is more than one theatre in London today where the pumps work night and day under the stage to hold them back.

The Wandle meandered from Wandsworth to Wimbledon, and was noted for its fine fishing and the surly insularity of its community of carp-breeders. Perhaps the most famous of all was the Tyburn River because it gave its name to the popular spectator sport of hanging on Tyburn Tree, where good seats could be obtained from Mammy Douglas at half-a-crown a time. The river emerged from the heights of Hampstead, flowed down through Swiss Cottage to Marble Arch (where the gibbet stood) to what is now Green Park, where it split into 'two-burns' forming the high mound of Thorney Island before foaming down to join the Thames.

A few centuries ago, therefore, you could hardly walk more than half a mile without getting your feet wet, and by the banks of these now long-vanished rivers, lived specialists who disappeared with them and whose titles have changed in meaning. The water-cress grower, the water-seller who roamed the streets with twopenny buckets of spring water, the 'tosher' who earned his living by crawling along the river under overhanging houses to retrieve the occasional lost child, wedding ring or moggie. A much respected professional was the scavenger, who, in addition to being a customs inspector, was responsible for keeping rights of way along towpaths clear, and had to deal with constant complaints from victims who had tripped over the mooring-lines of 'for hire' boatmen waiting for a fare, or curbing the habit of Smithfield market men and fishwives who were wont to throw the guttings into the river. Around London Bridge was another rather interesting little colony of corporation men who were responsible for keeping the stonework rendered and forestalled Wimpeys by several hundred years, for they were kitted with borough overalls and boots for the job. Intermingled with these were fiercely individual fishing families (some still using the ancient British coracle), who harvested netloads of gourmet, mops, sprats, pilchards, bream, lampreys, barbels and pike from home waters within sight of the Tower. Backing them, boat-builders of every kind, rope-makers, sail-makers and a dozen other craftsmen specialising in London's fishing industry.

However, it was from the port of London itself that most folk drew their living, and incidentally supplied a fine crop of occupational surnames – Porters, Cadwallenders, Coopers, Carpenters, Watermans, Turners, Salters, Chandlers, Wharfingers, Fishers and so on. As the merchants had formed themselves into powerful guilds to protect their monopolies, so did the watermen, who split into ferrymen, lightermen, sailormen, and pilots, but they were all united on one principle: they knew the value of their river, and their dependence on it, and what's more they knew the landsman's dependence upon them.

So many people were plying their trade upon the Thames during the sixteenth century that laws were passed by Parliament to regulate their conduct. Since the fifteenth century the law known as 'Deddand' had been in existence whereby the waterman's craft could be cut in half and the waterman forced to serve a term in the Royal Navy if his vessel was the cause of any accident on water, and the formation of Watermen and Lightermen's Hall in the 1550s guaranteed that the fraternity themselves exercised some control over the behaviour of their men. It had jurisdiction over all watermen between Windsor and Gravesend – the point where the old Saxon Portgereve's authority took over. To obtain the coveted licence to practise legally, an apprentice was elected, usually by fellow members, when his papers of indenture were cut in half. He kept one half, the Hall the other. There followed between five and seven years hard apprenticeship when the boy had to learn every twisting current and eddy of the upriver waters and how to handle the long 'sweeps' by which he propelled his vessel, under the constant supervision of overseers. Finally came a rigorous oral examination in front of a panel of his peers, and if he passed that, the other half of his indenture was returned, a number prescribed on his licence, and an arm-plate bearing the vow 'At command of our superiors' given to him.

In 1594, John Norden claimed that some 40,000 were employed directly on the river within the City limits alone, but this figure probably included every opportunist with a boat, including all the fishermen who worked upriver – all the unlicensed 'nonners' as they are still known by legitimate watermen to this day. Certainly throughout medieval and Elizabethan times familiar, long, low grumbles could be heard about the influx of foreigners undercutting trade, a grumble which periodically broke out in fierce riots. Within the fraternity, demarcations were clearly defined, and although a man might undertake several specialities, he had to carry a licence for each one. The true waterman carried passengers only. Lightermen carried goods not passengers, ferrying cargoes in their barges which 'lightened' trading vessels, and also transported goods from one shoreside warehouse to another by water. The wording of the waterman's licence remains the same today. He was licensed: "in the navigation of row boats, sailing boats, steam boats and vessels on all parts of the River Thames, from, and opposite to, and including Teddington Lock in the Counties of Middlesex and Surrey, to and opposite to, and including Lower Hope Point Gravesend, in the County of Kent, and in or on all Docks, Canals, Creeks and Harbours of, or out of, the said River, so far as the tide flows therein."

He was granted a number for this licence, 'which Licence and number have been duly registered as required by Law'. The lighterman was similarly licensed, but with the regulation that 'goods, wares or merchandise' were to be carried 'without passengers'. There were anomalies and special privileges, of course. The lightermen of Ware in Hertfordshire, for instance, were rewarded with automatic free rights from the days of the Great Plague when they brought in food and supplies to the quarantined City. And the legitimacy of taking passengers on a sailing barge whose skipper might have been a member of Watermen and Lightermen's Hall remained somewhat hazy.

Within the two main distinctions smaller, more exclusive specialists developed. Trinity House Men (known as hog grubbers) were allowed to handle special cargoes barred to other lightermen, and others formed the élite of the river pilots guiding large trading vessels safely from Gravesend to the Pool of London. Combined with these duties, was the responsibility of Watermen's Hall to provide the only efficient fire-fighting force London had, and in the

Shipping off Woolwich by Thomas Mellish.

A Turner water colour sketch, made between 1789–1802, offers a rare early picture of the Thames sailing barge's development, still with the Viking square sail.

days of the highly inflammable wattle and daub timber-framed houses which crowded the Thames shore, this vital function increased the City's dependence upon them.

In lesser or greater degrees of affiliation to Watermen's Hall, were those watermen who propelled their barges by sail and ventured much further eastwards than Gravesend, the limit of the Portgereve's authority. These men were the Thames sailing barge sailormen who combined the knowledge of upriver congestion with the sailmanship of the deep-sea mariner. Some took papers, others didn't, but they were all loosely related by the guidelines prescribed at Watermen's Hall, and in many cases, by family connections.

For the waterman working exclusively under the eyes of City institutions, more rigorous laws came into force. Complaints had been made of the 'rude, ignorant and unskilful numbers of watermen whereby diverse persons have been robbed and spoiled of their goods, and also drowned' earlier in the century, but with the formation of their own guild; legitimate members were more apt to fear the censure of their colleagues than the ancient Deddand laws, for their own clan punishments were much more severe than Parliament's. Later, a waterman's salty language was curbed by fines which could be as high as half-a-crown if his fare took exception.

Fierce demarcations existed on the water, but once any vessel's prow touched the quayside, even tighter cliques took over. Elizabeth I had designated twenty legal quays which were cleared by customs, and on them worked teams of specialists each with their own highly prized system of licensing. The Fellowship of Billingsgate Porters also unloaded coal, salt and corn. The Tacklehouse Porters, at the top of the ladder, handled measured freights and were equipped with weights and measures. The Companies' Porters monopolised all exports and imports from Holland, France, Spain, Italy, Germany and the Baltic. The Ticket Porters, who also enjoyed the Freedom of the City, handled exclusively those goods from the new colonies in America.

However, trade increased to such an extent that many ships could not get to the legal quays and had to lay at anchor in midstream, and the ranks of the lightermen increased, offloading goods in mid-stream, ship to shore, and to some extent breaking the Trinity House men's monopoly. Profits were high for the dock owner, and this practice laid the seeds for centuries of antagonism between the lightermen, watermen and sailormen and the quay operator. To add to the confusion, over the years the terminology became blurred and the term waterman became a convenient general designation for all licensed men who transported goods on water or ferried passengers up, down or over the Thames.

As specific demands changed the style of work, so the watermen's vessels were adapted to meet those demands, from the sailed barges of the sailormen, which bore a striking resemblance to the Viking longship, to the boxlike lighters, propelled by sweeps, or the diversity of the ferrymen's vessels.

If landsmen wished to cross the river they either had to use rickety, congested, old London Bridge, or they could hail a boatman. Westminster was also divided from the City by a belt of marshy or dangerous ground. It was not unknown for a sudden fog to descend and the hapless foot-slogger to find himself wallowing up to the armpits in reeds and river ooze or, worse, he might fall into the hands of marsh rats and lose his shirt. It was easier to pay up and ride

Watermen at Wapping Old Stairs, Rowlandson, 1807.

the distance by water from the Strand to Westminster.

The humbler ferryman stood aft in his small boat propelling it by describing a figure-of-eight motion with a single oar. There was the double-oared, and sometimes sailed hoy, named after the Norse word for 'stop'; the sculler which was hailed by shouting 'oars' (and caused much surprise amongst foreigners who found the riversider very brazen in calling out so loudly for what they took to be something else); and there were the six or eight-oared wherries about twenty feet long operated usually by a single family clan, for the richer traveller preferred to travel in comfort, as many of these vessels sported a canopy and soft cushions for the fare's behind. There were the little 'cocks', fast scudding boats operated by the Robinson clan of Bankside (which is why the Robinsons are known as 'cockies' to this day). Then there were the shallow 'punts' which manoeuvred up a dozen little inlets to deliver the fare to his door, and for the daredevil, those watermen who could 'shoot' the raging rapids which roared through the silted buttresses of London Bridge to drop some six feet into the calmer waters of the Pool below it.

Many of the rich had their personal wherries, together with their own landing places; there's one for example left high and dry in Charing Cross Gardens. The bishops also had the right to operate wherries for financial gain, which was a constant source of irritation to the watermen. One such was the Bishop of Lambeth who constantly undercut them between sermons on the value of thrift and honesty. The good sisters of St. Mary Overie also operated a flourishing ferry at Southwark. The Order was established by the daughter of a wealthy ferryman, who, it is said, in a misguided quest to see how popular he was, played dead. Unable to contain himself at the wake being celebrated downstairs on his behalf, he decided to take a peek below, and a terrified apprentice, thinking he was a ghost, slammed him over the head. So the hapless man joined his ancestors for real. The wherryman's daughter, filled with remorse, formed the Order, but with a characteristic eye for business we notice that she didn't give up her father's ferry.

It is from the first part of the seventeenth century that many of the families still working the London waters stem, their long ancestry traced through the numbered lists of licensed watermen preserved at Watermen and Lightermen's Hall, for so coveted were those hard-won papers, that in most cases, it was a natural progression for son to follow father. One such waterman working the Thames at this time was John Taylor, a self-educated man who became their early spokesman against 'nonners', and is best known as the waterman poet.

Taylor has left us some interesting pictures of his passengers from the type who would get in, sit still, pay up and leave without a murmur, to the passenger who, spending money 'on a whore, tobacco or Bacchus blood' with a waterman:

that hath rowed till his heart ache, and sweats till he hath not a dry thread about him, the gentleman's bounty is asleep, and he will pay him by the statute, or, if he give him twopence more, he hath done a huge work beyond the merit of Suttons Hospital . . . he hath never left off roaring, "row! row! row! A pox on you row!" . . . When landed where he pleases, he hath told me that I must wait upon him, and he will return to me presently, and I shall carry him back again and be paid altogether. Then I have attended for five or six hours (like John Noakes) for nothing, for my cheating shark having neither money nor honesty, hath never come at me, but took some other pair of oars, and in the same fashion cozened another waterman for his boat hire.

Like all watermen he would have been fully conversant with the Bankside whistle, for all waterside communities had identification signals, and Bankside had its shadier fraternities, not least of which were the brothels, or stews. Apart from the visiting medic going there to collect fine specimens from the leech beds which abounded the marshes, there was often the gentleman hopping over the water for a night on the tiles, eager to meet his 'Tomboy' or 'Punk' as the ladies were then known. Adding to the rich variety of fares, were the bear-baiting enthusiasts keen to watch Harry Huck and his champion grizzly at the Bear Gardens.

Like so many of his day, he drew a good living from the playgoers who flocked to Bankside to visit the Globe, Swan, Rose and Hope, and like all central watermen, enjoyed a friendly camaraderie with the players who congregated at the Cardinal's Hat nearby. Taylor might well have ferried the busy Shakespeare, or jovial Ben Jonson to Bull Alley Stairs. He might have swopped reminiscences with a playgoer on his way to see the new play *Tempest* which promised a lively rendition of a shipwreck based upon that of Sir George Somers and Richard Rich in the Bermudas in 1609. He might even have risked offering a sample of his own verse on the subject of imminent drowning in a vein which would certainly have raised a guffaw from the groundlings. The subject of this particular passage was a less well-endowed mate:

> Hall and his wife into the water slipt
> She quickly Hall's shaft by the codpiece gript.
> And reason good she had to catch him there,
> For hold the shaft, she need no drowning feare.
> She oft had try'd and prov'd and found it so,
> That thing would never to the bottome go!

To the watermen's horror, in 1613 the playhouses moved across to Middlesex and John Taylor was elected spokesman for the fraternity to petition King James against this. He recalled the great service done "in Queene Elizabeth's reigne, of famous memorie, in the voyage to Portingale, with the right honourable and never to be forgotten Earle of Essex [by] the Watermen, with their loss of lives and limbs to defend their Prince and Country". For good measure he reminded the monarch how they had:

served with Sir Francis Drake, Sir John Hawkins, Sir Martin Frobisher and others, in Cales action, and Iland voyage, in Ireland, Low Countries . . . 1,500 or 2,000 of them imployed having but nine shillings and foure pence the month a peece for theire pay . . . and forebeare to charging of their Prince for six or nine and twelve month . . . and all those great numbers of men remained at home; and the Players have all (except the Kings Men) left their usual residence in Bankside and doe play in Middlesex which art remote from the Thames, so that every day they do draw unto them three or four thousand people, that were used to spend their monies by water to the reliefe of so many thousands of poore people . . .

Despite this plea, the players did move, and a good deal of rancour was engendered between players and watermen as a result. Taylor had more than a hint of the showman in his own make-up, however, and the same year sees him stage-managing two pageants in celebration of the marriage of the King's daughter Elizabeth in 1613. Later, in 1620, he created much excitement when he bet other watermen that he and a vintner friend could sail a boat made of paper from the City to Queenborough on the Isle of Sheppey. He had advertised the spectacle extensively so that:

Thousands more did meet us with the tide,
With scullers, Oares, with ship-boats, and with
Barges to gaze on us . . .

Whether the watermen had got their heads together in order to do the retreating players one in the eye, is a nice thought. However, they hadn't gone very far in the makeshift boat when:

Our boat being female, began to leake,
Being as most vessels are most weak . . .

The water to the paper being got,
In one halfe hour, our boat began to rot.
The Thames (most librell) filled hér to the halves,
Whilst Hodge and I sate liquor'd to the Ealves . . .

Cunning as ever, Taylor had brought along a set of eight bullocks'
bladders which inflated in a Stuart version of the Mae West, and they
completed their journey to Queenborough, where the mayor feasted
the pair and the populace tore up the soggy mess, 'Wearing their
relicks in their hats and caps'.

Unlike most central watermen who tended not to venture too far
below London Bridge, and thus had only occasional contact with
sailormen from downriver reaches with their strange dialect of
Kentish Greenwich, or Greenhithe, Taylor travelled quite widely to
Europe and beyond, often skippering his own vessel, and through
his City waterman's eyes we get an interesting glimpse of the 'Wild
Saxon shore', land of the Western bargeman, as the wilderness was
still known. Bound for East Anglia he set sail in July 1622 equipping
himself with:

Sayles, with anker, cables, sculs and oares,
With cade and compasse, to know the sea and shores,
With lanthorne, candle, tinder-box and match.

Peter boat fishermen on Greenwich Marshes in the early nineteenth century.

He sailed downstream past Rotherhithe with its brotherhood of
pilots who prayed for shipwrecked mariners, past Greenwich

marshes where a small colony of watermen and fishermen lived in isolation, past the pig farms of Charlton, the Isle of Dogs with its fishing village, past small gunpowder plants dotting the shoreline to Gravesend and beyond .

> . . . rowing down stream,
> And near to Lee, we to an Anchor came.
> Because the sandes were bare, and water low,
> We rested there, till it two houres did flow . . .
> Where 30 miles we passed, a mile from shore,
> The water two feet deep, or little more.
> Thus past we on to the brave East Saxon coast,
> From 3 am morne, till two of noone almost,
> By Shoebury, Eakering, Fowleness, Tittingham,
> And then we into deeper water came.
> There is a crooked Bay runnes winding fare,
> To Maulden, Esterford and Colchester . . .

John Taylor lived on into the troubled reign of Charles I and was one of the watermen who petitioned for peace between Parliament and the King to the House of Lords in 1648. When the Civil War raged he went off to the Royalist headquarters, Oxford, returning to open a pub in Phoenix Alley off Long Acre which he dedicated to the beheaded Charles I, insolently calling it the Mourning Crown. However, even his friends thought this was going a bit too far, and persuaded him to change it to the Poet's Head. He never lost his, dying there in 1653 of natural causes.

Let us leave the waterman poet with the last word on his beloved river – and a prophetic word at that, concerning a problem which was to grind the Houses of Parliament to a halt three centuries later.

> Great in goodnesse is the River Thames,
> From whose diurnall and nocturnal flood,
> Millions of souls have fuel, cloathes and food;
> . . . of Watermen, their servants, children and wives,
> It doth maintaine, near twenty-thousand lives . . .
> What doth it do, but give our full contents?
> Brings food, and for it takes our excrements.
> Yields us all plenty, worthy of regard,
> And dirt, and muck we give it for reward?

Muck and Brass

Filthy river, filthy river,
Foul from London to the Nore
What art thou but one vast gutter,
One tremendous common shore.

Punch

ONE GREAT UPRIVER tradition which has survived to this day from the eighteenth century is the annual race for Doggett's Coat and Badge. Emphasising the once deep alliance between watermen and players, Thomas Doggett, who had been a leading player with the Drury Lane Theatre company, instituted a race in 1715 to be run by six young watermen within a year of ending their apprenticeships. It was rowed from the Swan at London Bridge to the Swan at Chelsea on the first Monday in August (in 1777 the course was reversed). When he died in 1721 he bequeathed a sum of money each year for the race. A bright orange coat and silver badge bearing the rampant horse of Hanover in celebration of George I's monarchy is presented annually to the winner. Preparations for the race were an opportunity for prolonged festivities. It is interesting to hear Charles Dickens' account of the days when a competitive race on the water was attended by immense crowds and traditional way-gunfiring a century later:

> The water is studded with boats of all sorts, kinds and descriptions; places in the coal barges at the different wharfs are let to crowds of spectators, beer and tobacco flow freely about; men, women and children

wait for the start with breathless expectation; cutters of six and eight oars glide gently up and down, waiting to encourage their protégés during the race; bands of music add to the animation if not the harmony of the scene, groups of watermen at different stairs discussing the merits of the respective candidates; and the prize wherry which is rowed slowly about is an object of general interest.

Two O'Clock strikes . . . a gun is heard, and a noise of distant huraa'ing along each bank of the river – every head is bent forward – the noise draws nearer and nearer: 'Go on Pink!' – 'Give it to 'er Red' – 'Sullivan for ever!' . . . 'Now Tom! Now! Why dontcher stretch out?' – 'Two pints to a pot on Yellow!' Every little public house fired its gun and hoisted a flag.

The race for Doggett's Coat and Badge probably changed little over the centuries, but everyday life for the riverside dweller changed considerably as the years wore on. At the beginning of the eighteenth century Bermondsey was still a small hamlet where the Church and richer laity had built country retreats and where they strolled along Halfpenny Hatch near the Surrey Canal which was noted for its 'singing birds, snipe, moorhen, kingfishers and wild duck and geese in season'. People still pickled herrings in Pickle Herring Street and whalers unloaded their catch at Greenland Dock. London, which Hippolyte Taine was describing as a 'Cyclops', was spreading slowly and steadily in every direction; trade was growing, the population expanding and the numbers of houses and docks being built increasing, but the great explosion had not yet arrived. As the eighteenth century gave way to the nineteenth, however, the speed of change became more rapid, culminating in the chaos of the industrial revolution.

At first the boom meant more work for watermen. There were contracts to carry over twenty million bricks in 1800 alone. Towards Limehouse Reach, traditionally an area for lime refining, the West India Dock was begun in 1802 for the handling of sugar, rum and coffee – first an import basin, then an export basin, with more land swallowed later for the South Dock. At the southern end of the Isle of Dogs where once three families of watermen had lived in isolation, the rural inhabitants of Millwall, with its several little windmills, waited to be engulfed in turn by Millwall Docks. In 1805 there was London Docks for the wool and wine trade; two years later saw the opening of the Surrey and the Commercial Docks where the whalers were to give way to softwood, deal and other timbers, a pond seventy acres in area for floating timbers opening in 1807. Little St. Katharine's dealt in the finer cargoes of china, ivory and carpets, its dockers carrying on the skilled traditions of the medieval porters and bearing numbered discs on their arms to admit them into the Aladdin's cave of wine, tobacco and finery. Something of the Gold Rush fervour can be seen in the haste with which St. Katharine's Dock was constructed in 1827. Eleven thousand three hundred people living there were dispossessed and only lease and freeholders were compensated as 1,250 houses were pulled down, so great was the fever to expand trade. Even St. Katharine's hospital, endowed since the twelfth century and supposedly under the protection of George IV, was demolished, the coffins being rather indecently turfed up and dumped elsewhere. The complete dock with warehouses was in operation in twelve months, and the tentacles of tenements began to meet up with those of London Docks so that one could no longer differentiate one community from another.

On the other side of the river, watermen living near Greenland watched as first one dock, then another was added, and at first were no doubt pleased by the additional fares this brought them daily, as armies of labourers hired them to get to and from work across the river. By 1819 six bridges had been built across the Thames above London Bridge which slowly whittled away the upriver watermen's monopoly. But although alarming stories reached the Greenland men via redundant cousins upriver, they hardly imagined a bridge would arrive to put them out of business. They were still innocent of the ingenuity of men like Marc and Isambard Brunel, until in 1825 the labourers arrived to build the brick kilns which would signal the Rotherhithe tunnel – the Great Bore as it was known – a two passage connection which housed fine shops specialising in jewellery. The excitement soon waned however, and the gentry stopped visiting, so that it degenerated into a meeting place for prostitutes and card sharps. A community of 350 watermen who had previously ferried some 3,700 people daily between Rotherhithe and Wapping watched their livelihood vanish and were driven back before the huge army of immigrant labour which arrived via the tunnel to settle on the southern banks.

Many traditional festivals disappeared at this time, like the water procession of craft decorated by wives and girls of the neighbourhood which once sculled downriver to Rotherhithe with accompanying cannon and trumpets on each Trinity Monday in celebration of the pilots of London. Deep-sea connections survived only as names in the registers of churches like St. Nicholas's with its vestry designed like a ship's cabin: proud seafaring names like Peter Pett, inventor of the frigate; Drake's captain, Jonas Shish; Edward Fenton and George Shevlocke who navigated the globe; and Frobisher who searched for the North-West Passage.

In less than a generation, rural villages which had every reason to believe they'd stay that way for ever, were overrun by alien city values, violent crime, sweat shops and steam. Inlets which ten years before had yielded sea-food to supplement meagre incomes were awash with filth. Add to this the riversiders' deep-rooted feeling that they were being misrepresented 'up there' by a Parliament who gave not a damn for them, and overall by a King who seemingly returned their years of service to the Crown in the Napoleonic Wars with indifference. In one case a group of seasoned Trafalgar veterans on coast-guard were casually disbanded on a Sussex hill in the middle of winter, miles from home, without any back pay. Stir in a huge influx of foreign labour which undercut the local man, and an arsenal at Woolwich which periodically exploded in their faces, and you have the ingredients of a very hard morsel which was bound to leave successive generations with a lump in its throat.

Many people 'swallowed the anchor', emigrated, or moved further south; others worked on the theory 'if you can't beat 'em join 'em', and stayed to adapt their skills to the industrial age, becoming boilermakers and engineers on the new steam tugs and dockside machinery. Many simply took the philosophical view and adapted old methods to the new age. The ship builders of Deptford and Blackwall who had built the great 'wooden walls' and Armada warships (which in a painting by Francis Holman fifty years before had depicted no less than thirteen ships on the slips in a busy yard surrounded by bleak nothing), soon found that the river was too narrow to launch the new, much larger vessels, so they broke up into small firms of perhaps one or two families and became specialists in river craft such as lighters and wherries, or the smaller coastal sailing barges. Some fell to repairing vessels, and some to adapting craft from sail to steam. Blackwall built sail-vessels like the *Cutty Sark* which could outstrip anything else on the fast tea-clipper runs. Others, philosophically accepting change, turned their hands to breaking up the sailing vessels which had served them so well, ironically adapting the timber for railway sleepers. Early one overcast day in 1838, the artist Turner set up his easel at Cherry Garden Pier near Bermondsey to capture for all time the paradox of the age, as the once mighty fighting *Temeraire* lurched with sails stripped under the smoking stacks of steam tugs to be unceremoniously broken up in John Beatson's Yard.

To get some idea of the speed of expansion, take the 630 acres of Greenwich Marshes which had for years been cut off by the natural barriers of perilous ditches and inlets. In 1841 it housed only 514 people, mostly of Kentish stock, with twelve Protestant Irishmen, and George Adamson, a Scottish rope-maker. There were two fishermen, five watermen, two lightermen, a river-pilot, one seaman, and nine market-gardeners. By 1851 there were several more rope-makers for the new Enderby's Wharf, and workers at the boilermaking company there, several more agricultural labourers, mostly from far afield, brought in to handle the increased demand for vegetables from upriver. In 1861 they were joined by 187 Irish labourers – Catholics mostly, who found themselves in a staunchly Protestant area. Rough housing was erected at Marsh Lane, Hatcliffe Street, and the Lower Woolwich Road, and the ghetto system which scarred Whitechapel and Hoxton arrived here. By 1863, one hundred of these Irish labourers had found their way into 'Spike' – the Union Workhouse at Greenwich, and the local priest, Father Wallace, was saying that his congregation did not attend mass because they were ashamed to be seen crossing Greenwich Park in their rags; or more probably for fear of some extreme Protestants who for years had traditionally burnt effigies of the Pope at Angersteins' Wharf nearby each Guy Fawkes night, and saw their scapegoats in these unhappy people.

The new bridges across the Thames created a new waterside profession, that of tipstaff or toll-taker, sitting there in his small watch hut at the bridge threshold, a good fire brazier beside him in winter and his lead tray for coins – a halfpenny on weekdays and a penny on Sundays. It wasn't until 1879 when the Prince and Princess of Wales zigzagged ceremoniously over Lambeth, Vauxhall, Victoria, Albert and old Chelsea bridges that they were declared 'free and open to the public for ever', and the communities on either side of the river were enabled to mingle more easily than ever before. But until that time toll-keepers were an intransigent lot, as is clear from a story told by lighterman Harry Thomas Harris who recorded his memories of the river in a few notebooks before he died. Before the advent of the railway Harry Thomas Harris's grandfather walked to Brentford from Southwark to bring a barge downriver. Upon his arrival, he discovered he had forgotten the toll money. So he walked back to Southwark, obtained the tolls, and strolled up to Brentford again to come away the following tide to row the barge down to London – a walk of seven miles each time.

The toll-keeper was something of a connoisseur when it came to suicide, for they were constantly retrieving 'stiffs' from the river: ladies float face up, gents float face down, ran the legpull. One was effusive on the subject to the young Dickens:

'Suicide! Is that what yer want ter know about? I've seen a good deal of that work I can assure yer! Likely enough with women . . . there's adeal of trouble about you see . . . one time a young woman come from Blackfriars and crosses 12 o'clock in the open day . . . got through onto Waterloo and before I gets to er, she darts over the parapet . . . shot herself over the side . . . Watermen awf . . . lucky escape . . . clothes bound her up . . . alarm given. This is the best place! If people jump off straight forwards from the middle of the parapet of the bays of the bridge, they don't kill themselves drowning, but are smashed, poor blighters . . . that's what they are . . . they dash 'emselves upon the buttress of the bridge. But *you* jump awf from the *side* of the bay, and you'll tumble true into the stream under the arch . . . what you've got to do is mind *how* you jump in! There was poor Tom Steele from Stamford Street (Southwark) . . . didn't dive! Bless you, didn't dive at all! Fell down flat into the water –he broke his breast-bone . . . lived two days! . . . They got all kinds of reasons . . .'

Reasons many of them had for sure. Dispossessed in their own traditional crafts by a hundred and one mechanical inventions, from the Highlands of Scotland to the crofts of Cornwall, desperate families streamed to London to find that the gold at the end of the rainbow consisted of lean-to shacks in the shanty towns which now squatted the marshes between the City and Westminster, and straddled the slums of Southwark. The choice for many lay between suicide and the workhouse.

The Poor Law Reform Act of 1836 gave the Number 1 dietary for a working man as: first 3 days: 12 ounces bread, 1½ pints of gruel, 5 ounces cooked meat, 1½ pounds potatoes, and 1½ pints of broth; with (if the rations ever penetrated the rich rind of graft at the

Spikes) 12 ounces bread, 2 ounces cheese, for the next three days and on Fridays 1½ pints gruel and 14 ounces of suet.

In 1801 the population of London was under a million but within fifty years it had swelled to over two and a quarter million. To some this growth meant success and money; indeed it was the commercial heyday for the sailing barge owners, but to others it meant the fundamental destruction of insular traditions on the waterfront. Worst of all the huge population and spreading industry brought muck, disease and foul waters. Hopelessly inadequate cess-pits overflowed freely into the river. Among the husbandmen and small farmers who remained downriver, some managed to make a virtue of affliction by gathering human manure from lay-stalls for their crops.

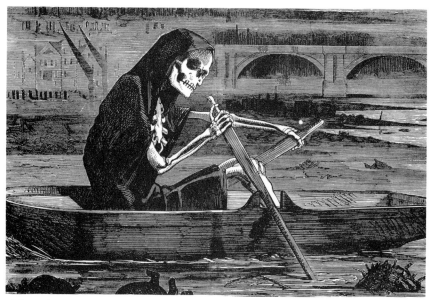

The 'silent highway'-man. 'Your money or your life.' An eloquent contemporary comment on the Great Stink of 1858.

By 1832, 'King Cholera' had claimed more than 40,000 lives in three epidemics. Working watermen were keeling over in the fumes, and the stench from the river was so suffocating that Members of Parliament were having to resort to nose-masks and chloride-of-lime-soaked curtains in the House. Yet, despite such a ripe example of 'Monster Soup' right under their noses, few members supported any action. Meanwhile, some people went to see for themselves the conditions in which thousands lived. In 1837, Charles Dickens wandered the streets of 'Cholera Capital', as the riverside slum was known, as he made his notes for *Oliver Twist*.

Near to that part of the Thames where the buildings on the banks are dirtiest, and the vessels on the river blackest with the dust of colliers, and the smoke of low-roofed houses, there exists the filthiest, the strangest, the most extraordinary of the many localities that are hidden in London, unknown even by name, to the great mass of its inhabitants. To reach this place, penetrate through a maze of narrow muddy streets, thronged by the roughest and poorest waterside people. The coarsest and commonest articles of wearing apparel strewn from the house parapet and windows. Jostling with unemployed labourers of the lowest class, ballast heavers, coal-whippers, brazen women, ragged children, and the very raff and refuse of the river. In such a neighbourhood, beyond dockhead in the borough of Southwark, stands Jacob's Island surrounded by a muddy ditch, six or eight feet deep and fifteen or twenty feet wide when the tide is in, once called Mill Pond, but known in these days as Folly Ditch. Crazy wooden warehouses with holes from which to look upon the slime beneath, dirt and squalor thrusting itself out above the mud, and threatening to fall into it. Dirt besmeared walls and decaying foundations; every repulsive lineament of poverty, every loathsome indication of filth, rot and garbage – all these ornament the banks of Folly Ditch.

To which one alderman who worked on the theory 'out of sight out of mind' retorted that no such place existed. The position worsened so that by 1849 we have this letter to *The Times* – a pathetic memorial signed by fifty-four desperate people:

Sur,
May we beg and beseech your proteckshion and power. We are, Sur, as it may be, livin in a Wilderness, so far as the rest of London knows anything of us, or as the rich and great people care about. We live in muck and filthe. We ain't got no privez, no dust bins, no drains, no water splies, and no drain or suer in the whole place. The Suer Company, in Greek Street, Soho Square, all great, rich and powerfool men, take no notice watsomedever of our complaints. The stenche of a Gully-hole is disgustin. We al of us suffur, and numbers are ill, and if the Cholera comes Lord help us . . .

In June 1858, Mother Thames hit as hard as she could with 'The Great Stink' as it was known, and Parliament almost ground to a complete halt. This time the House was prepared to listen to the pleas for action from Disraeli and other reformers, though many still felt that the threepence on the rates which any clean-up campaign would necessitate was politically imprudent. *The Times* stubbornly claimed, 'We prefer to take our chance with cholera and the rest, than be bullied into health.' Luckily for upriver, bullies did exist, and a year later Joseph Bazelgate had pushed his outfall sewer through the maze.

Indicating yet one more difference between rich and poor communities, collectors of trivia noted with interest that the highest flow of sewerage from the West End occurred three hours later than from the East End. However, time differentials did not interest the inhabitants of Woolwich who were more concerned at the filth where the new outfall sewer disgorged. Ships could no longer stock with drinking water there as they had done for centuries, and Barking fishing folk drew up netloads of poisoned fish.

Doggett's Coat and Badge watermen launching their racing gig at the Anchor and Hope in 1958.

4

The Hulks

So it's bad luck to you Judges and Jurors,
Justice and Old Bailey too,
Seven years I am sent from my true love,
Seven years upon Botany Bay . . .

Song

ONE ASPECT OF Charlton riverside life which persisted for several hundred years was the presence of convict labour. Parliament had found itself with an overflowing prison system in the seventeenth century. Someone had the bright idea of transporting felons to the colonies in America. Since, by the late eighteenth century, the colonies had the pick of voluntary émigrés (many of whom were glad enough to escape the encroaching London slums), they refused any more transportees, and when the War of Independence broke out, the transport vessels were moored round the bend at Woolwich and Deptford to await the hopefully victorious outcome, when business would recommence as usual. Unhappily the war was not won, and the river was left with several vessels crowded with the poor wretches. The moored hulk became an integral part of the penal system, with, by 1782, a human cargo of 1017 prisoners. A certain Duncan Campbell was paid to look after three vessels moored at Woolwich, where successive prison hulks ended their days, rotting and fever ridden.

It must have become an everyday occurrence for working watermen, their apprentices, children and barge wives drying the washing, to see the convicts at work on shore where they were employed in shifting ballast, digging trenches and sawing timbers for the dock extensions.

By the early part of the nineteenth century, transportation had started again, this time to New South Wales, but the hulks themselves had now become permanent, and anyone hapless enough to be condemned to one knew they were not going anywhere, although transport ships did still embark from Woolwich. The hulks became a popular tourist attraction to the disgust, I would think, of local people who lived closer to the inmates as they worked off the Warren. Many local lightermen were directly engaged in ballast work with the convicts and would have been able, by this day-to-day contact, to put a name to a face, and although most of the convicts were 'foreigners' from other parts of the country, it is difficult to imagine the waterfront workers at Hunter Gregory's Coal Yard viewing the poor wretches with anything but sympathy for they knew well that a man could be transported or 'hulked' for such a small offence as scratching the woodwork on Chelsea Bridge. I imagine they looked at them with a good deal of 'there but for the grace of God go I . . .'

Convicts from the hulks being employed near Woolwich, 1779.

The locals would have been totally familiar with scenes such as Magwitch's escape in *Great Expectations*, for any fleeing prisoner had only one practical avenue of retreat, the countryside beyond Charlton or Blackheath. An up-countryman or townsman could not be expected to know the local bargeman's technique of paddling along the bottom of deep crevices in the marshes with a camouflaging canopy of overhanging marsh grass to conceal himself (a handy way to bag pheasants). Anyway, to do this the escaper would have had to swim the Thames in an age when very few watermen, let alone landsmen could swim! If he made west along the river he ran into the Arsenal troops. That left Charlton, and on more than one occasion, I suspect, the local people had stiffened as the 'escape' guns fired, staring sympathetically out of the windows as the torches of the troops combed the marsh in raking sweeps, whistles blowing from all corners. The mud-spattered convict, his lungs torn with effort, manacles flaying his skin, was probably struggling to reach the high ground of Cox's Mount and the gravel pits, beyond which lay trees and merciful shelter.

The following, described in a contemporary newspaper, was no doubt witnessed by many Charlton people in May 1832. It shows the desperate measures some would go to in order to get away from the hulks:

On Saturday afternoon a party of convicts were employed in Woolwich Dockyard in the charge of an officer and military sentinel. Four most determined characters named Boutel, Wallace, Dalton and Bannon suddenly rushed upon the sentinel . . . on duty at the west gate, and forcibly took away his rifle . . . on breaking into the London Road, the convicts betook themselves to the brickfields on the other side. Their ignorance of the localities induced them to climb a steep hill on the centre of Charlton sandpits . . . finding a ravine of great depth between them and the only spot by which they could expect to escape, they rapidly descended in full view of the excavators into the pits. Boutel, abandoning the rifle to Bannon, heavily chained as he was, and compelled to employ one hand in holding his fetters, squatted down, and folding his arms over his knees, rolled himself, bounding like a ball, down a steep precipice full 80 feet deep . . . the others passed through an orchard and some gardens, greatly alarming the inhabitants of that rural and retired spot, Woodland Place, who shut themselves in and watched the chase . . . the villains . . . were marched back to Woolwich. On board the hulks they were severely flogged.

A year later, stories reached the community of the fate of some transported felons, 108 female convicts and twelve children who had set sail for the prison settlement of New South Wales in the *Amphitrite* from Woolwich on August 25th, 1833. The vessel hit terrible gales off Boulogne harbour at three o'clock on the 30th and by four thirty had stuck on the sands. Thus far, mariners would have agreed the matter was simply a bad turn of the weather, something any local man on the coastal run could understand as 'fate', but what followed was against the oldest code of the sea and must have outraged many a sailorman.

The ship's surgeon, a Mr. Forester, seems to have defied his captain by ordering off the long boat, and the surgeon's wife is said "to have proposed to leave the convicts there, and go on shore without them" . . . "The female convicts who were battened down under the hatches of the vessel running aground broke away the half-deck hatch, and frantic, rushed upon the deck. Of course, they entreated the captain and surgeon to let them go on shore in the long boat, but they were not listened to, as the captain and the surgeon did not feel authorised to liberate prisoners committed to their care. About seven o'clock the flood tide began. The crew, seeing that there were no hopes, clung to the rigging. The poor 108 women and twelve children remained on deck uttering the most piteous cries. The vessel was about three-quarters of a mile from the shore – no more. Owen, one of the men saved, thinks that the women remained on deck in this state for about an hour and a half . . . Rice, a third man, floated ashore on a ladder. At the moment all the females disappeared, the ship broke in two" . . . "Body after body has been brought in. More than sixty have been found; they will be buried tomorrow. But alas! Alas! After all our efforts only three lives are saved out of 136." (The three lives were Owen, Rice and Towsey, the crewmen.)

The hulks were replaced from time to time. Captain Cook's proud *Discovery* ended her days in this ignominious role. *Reception*, which acted as a hospital ship was joined by *Justitia* housing 256 convicts, *Censor* with 250, and the *Retribution* with 600, notorious for the brutality of its guards. Another hulk, *The Morley*, lay off Galleon's Reach, with female convicts. On committal, a prisoner was billeted on the lower deck, presumably the worst place to be, with its stagnant bilges and mosquitoes, but with luck, or no doubt a little bribery, or 'garnish' as it was known, he could work himself to the middle, and then the upper deck, which could hardly have been the Ritz either.

Attendant disease was rife, and many epidemics spread to the community ashore. Just four death certificates for 1849 tell their own story.

8 Feb. 1849   John Morris – Male – 45 yrs – Convict: Apoplepsy of the Lungs

9 Feb. 1849   George Gallant – Male – 22 yrs – Convict: Tyhpus (5 days)

14 Mar. 1849   Wlm. Robinson – Male – 22 yrs – Convict: Ulceration of the Lungs (6 months)

14 Mar. 1849   Samuel Attwood – Male – 60 yrs – Convict: Dyarrhaea (3 weeks)

Local stories pervade of the inhuman way in which corpses of convicts were left on the hatches, sometimes partially dissected, for there was a lucrative traffic to the medical schools. The corpses were eventually rowed unceremoniously to the Arsenal wharf where they were buried in unmarked graves all over Plumstead marshes. Subsequent excavations have revealed skeletons, some of them still in chains, and tenants of all those semis now built over Plumstead way would do well to ponder the possibility of a grisly find when they're mulching over the rhubarb.

Thomas Dunscombe M.P. was finally prevailed upon by some influential prisoners to conduct a full enquiry, which found the system 'utterly disgraceful to a civilised and Christian country'. Despite this verdict the hulks *Warrior*, *Defence* and *Unite* remained until 1857. But the legacy does not end there. For whilst some were burned at Woolwich, others wallowed round Port Victoria and Queenborough as coal-hulks for many years more, and it is likely that their rotting keels are still to be seen.

The hulks left their mark on the downriver sailorman, for their involuntary waterside inhabitants were for many years an integral part of the riverside scene.

The following extract from a hulk register gives some indication of the mass exodus from north and south to London in the nineteenth century, for significantly, not one of the initialled names is a local-born man. These new waterfront dwellers had moved to London, dispossessed by the advent of the industrial revolution and its new demands. Often incarcerated for relatively trivial offences

The prison hulks off Woolwich, a rare photograph of 1851.

(seven years for bagging a pheasant) they found themselves condemned to a prison hammock, to sway for years in a sickening
tide-current, and wonder what went wrong in a new world turned
upside down by internal combustion. Probably there was the out
and out rogue in their number who had dodged the gibbet, but many
were starving, jobless country boys.

Name	Position in Institution	Age	Rank/Profession or occupation	Where Born
Y.J.	Convict	21	Painter	Lancs. Liverpool
J.L.	Convict	26	Labourer	Warwicks. Hillam
W.M.	Convict	31	do	Sussex. Bascombe
Y.C.	Convict	34	do	Hereford. Bedenham
C.F.	Convict	21	Brickmaker	Lincs. Wigtoft
J.W.	Convict	36	do	do. do.
G.B.	Convict	21	Tallow Chandler	Somerset. Chard
R.W.	Convict	14	Sawyer	do. Bishops Hill
W.E.	Convict	20	Labourer	Devon. Plymouth
H.C.	Convict	31	Sweep	Herts. Rickmansworth
W.E.	Convict	20	Labourer	do. Bracket Wood
J.H.	Convict	18	do	Somerset. Banwell
J.B.	Convict	25	Groom	Yorks. Sheffield
E.B.	Convict	22	Labourer	Norfolk. Montford
R.M.	Convict	27	Baker	Scotland. Dundee
T.W.	Convict	22	Labourer	Sussex. Allenbourne
W.J.P.	Convict	26	do	Devon. Exeter

Times were rough and no easier for people at Charlton than any other working community, so the meat-ration and other little perks received by prisoners caused a hardening of attitudes amongst law-abiding people ashore. Even to the most steely folk, however, the hulks and transports with their sorry human cargoes, and the ghoulish sightseers from the city, still there in an age which was supposed to be enlightened and liberal must have made a strange equation with progress. Almost a symbol of this two-sided morality was Mr. Bossey who was charged with mismanagement of the hulks, after Dunscombe's enquiry. Not two years before he had endowed a tidy sum for the Alms Houses of Rope-Yard Rails, which ironically were to become the breeding ground for violent street gangs later on.

There is a red-flowered nettle which grows along the marshes near the Arsenal, which is still known as 'the convicts' flower'. The nettle only grows on ground which has been turned and since the felon's grave is the only earth likely to be dug over there, the connection is clear. A carved bone dog sits staring over Charlton Heights to the Warren from my Aunt Anne's window-sill. It was made by a hulk prisoner and found its way into a riverside house, where many years later it was swopped for a handful of glass marbles by neighbour Jay to my father.

Grandad had a natural sympathy for others' hardship and once, rather mysteriously, said to me that if ever I was in trouble with the law, it was to the marshes I should make, for I could live off them indefinitely, and 'they' would never find me. He showed me the artful system of hidden planks which traversed the maze of winding dykes, mud flats, moving sands and ditches lacing that whole Kentish peninsula, the Hundred of Hoo, bounded by the Thames and the Medway. The run-in with the law, happily, never came, but I grew up knowing the marshes like the back of my hand.

Once in 1953, I had stood with Grandad on the foreshore, and watched two great sailing barges nosing into the mud-holes of Yantlet Creek, loaded down with concrete slabs. They had been winched ashore for the gangs of waiting labourers to hammer into place. The labourers were dressed in navy-blue and had bright orange triangles on their jackets. They were all convicts. So it isn't hard for me when I'm reading *Great Expectations* to relate to the passages in that great book, especially where:

> something clicked in the convict's throat, and he turned to the guard. The boat was rowed by a crew of chained convicts like himself. No one seemed surprised to see him, or interested in seeing him, or spoke a word, except that somebody in the boat growled 'give way, you!' which was the signal to dip oars. By the light of the torches, we saw the black hulk lying a little way in the mud off the shore, like a wicked Noah's Ark. Cribbed and moored by massive rusty chains, the prison ship seemed in my young eyes to be ironed like the prisoners. We saw the boat taken up the side and disappear. Then, the ends of the torches were flung hissing into the water, and went out, as if it were all over for him . . .

Thames barge unloading stone slabs for rebuilding the sea wall at Allhallows after the 1953 floods.

Sail and Steam

It's steam, boys, steam!
And things are not what they seem!
Though they roar and they bellow to frighten a fellow,
It's steam, lads, steam.

Broadsheet ballad

CHARLES DICKENS UNDERSTOOD the Thames and wrote of it as few other novelists have been capable. Apart from the haunting evocation of the hulks, he also draws in *Great Expectations* a fine picture of what the Pool of London looked like at its period of transition from sail to steam in the mid-nineteenth century.

At that time the steam traffic on the Thames was far below the present extent, and the watermen's boats were far more numerous. Of barges, sailing colliers, and coasting traders there was perhaps as many as now, but of steam ships not a tithe or twentieth part so many. Early as it was there were plenty of scullers about, and barges dropping down with the tide, and we went ahead amongst skiffs and wherries . . . old London Bridge, and Billingsgate with its oyster boats and Dutchmen, and the White Tower and traitor's gate: Here were the Leith and Aberdeen and Glasgow steamer loading and unloading goods, here colliers by the score, with coal-whippers plunging off stages on the decks as counterweights of coal swung up, which were then rattled over the side into barges . . . among the tiers of shipping in and out avoiding rusty chain cables, frayed hempen hawsers, and bobbing buoys, sinking for the moment floating baskets, scattering floating chips of wood and shavings, cleaving floating scum of coal, in and out under the figure-head of the *John of Sutherland* . . . and the *Betsy* of Yarmouth, with a firm formality of bosom and her nobby eyes starting two inches out of her head, in and out, hammers going in ship-builders' yard, saws going in leaky ships, capstans going . . . and unintelligible sea-creatures roaring curses over the bulwarks at respondent lightermen . . .

The change from sail to steam created dozens of new trades on the waterfront. Spheres of operation were now clear. Above the Customs post at Gravesend there were precise reaches, carefully documented and presided over by a bevy of pilots, tugmen and lightermen. A reach was, and still is, the maximum distance a sailing vessel could travel on one tack. Downriver was the land of the 'carrot crunchers' or 'chalkies' as the upalong lightermen termed all Kentish and Essex sailormen. The chalkies not only carried chalk to lighten Essex clay soils, but also to help reinforce the river banks and build barge hards. Forming a hyphen between the two were sailormen from Greenwich, the shape of their barges adapted to a dozen different purposes, who plied far upriver into the shallow creeks and marshes of Kent and Essex, and across the Channel to supply London with cargoes ranging from rough ballast and glass cullet, to fine wines and beer. Their barges were rightly known as the river pack horses. Congestion almost inconceivable when we look at today's solitary tug or wallowing lighter was described by Hippolyte Taine, a foreign visitor of the 1870s.

> From Greenwich the river is nothing but a street a mile broad and upwards, where ships ascend and descend between two rows of buildings, interminable rows of dull red, in brick and tiles bordered with great piles stuck in the mud for mooring vessels, which come here to load and unload . . . to the West rises an inextricable forest of yards, of masts, of rigging.

For four miles from London Bridge to Deptford the forest was continuous, sometimes up to 2,000 vessels in the river at any one time, and even as late as 1896 40% of that traffic was still sail.

From the wide racing currents and deserted marshland inlets of the estuary, Kent on the port, Essex to starboard, unknown to most mariners save the little fishing vessels and bargemen, the river meandered to Gravesend, the first sign of any large habitation, the place where land, as opposed to mud and marsh, met the sea. Here the Portgereve's authority took over. Here all visiting dignitaries were met and transported by 'long ferry' to London. Here incoming vessels took on a river pilot and had to get a clean bill of health, known as 'free pratique'. It was the last point where newborn babies of emigrants could be baptised. In 1840 there was a move to rename Gravesend First Port, but it never caught on, and the bawley men preferred their own nickname, Shrimp, from their fine quality local catches. After Gravesend came Northfleet Hope, St. Clement's Reach Greenhithe where some of the best sailormen came from, the long stretch past Dartford in Long Reach, then Erith Reach, Halfway Reach to Cross Ness, Barking Reach, twisting perilously again at Galleon's Reach known as the Devil's Elbow, perhaps a few cousins to shout to at Charlton and Woolwich Reach, then twist again for Bugsby's Reach; the name's origin was unclear, some said Bugsby was a lighterman, others that it derived from the bogs and the ghostly gases there. The river narrowed and tempers frayed as traffic built up into Blackwall Reach, the stately façade of Greenwich Palace as Greenwich Reach was manoeuvred, twist again for Lime-house Reach, serried ranks of timbers on the wharfside of the Surrey and Commercial Docks; to port in Tower Reach, the bellowing in the foreign cattle market to starboard, with its memories of 'the gibbet's tassel' and rotting bodies hanging at Execution Dock for three tides, and the carrot cruncher was in the thick of the land of the 'Goozer', the London waterman.

Surrounded by a sudden cacophony of noise and unfamiliar dialect, the Southwark lighterman, Harry Thomas Harris, as late as the 1890s found it almost impossible to converse with an Essex Western bargeman, as the Coastal men were mysteriously called.

With such an enormous traffic on the upriver Thames a man could specialise more or less exclusively, there being enough work to go round, but only if he 'got the eye', kept his nose clean (which in many cases meant not rocking his or anybody else's boat by complaining of low wages and the percentage demanded by the contractor in graft) and if he was prepared to see a job through, even if it meant seventy-two hours on the trot. Woe betide the lighterman who walked out on an unfinished job, however long it took. He was 'on the stones' and subject to a long period of discipline from the contractors. Nothing nearly as harsh as the 'calling on' system of the dockers though, but you minded your p's and q's nonetheless, and avoided contact with 'the nonners', those unlicensed freebooters so called to this day.

The lighterman's vessel was an offshoot of the sailing barge,

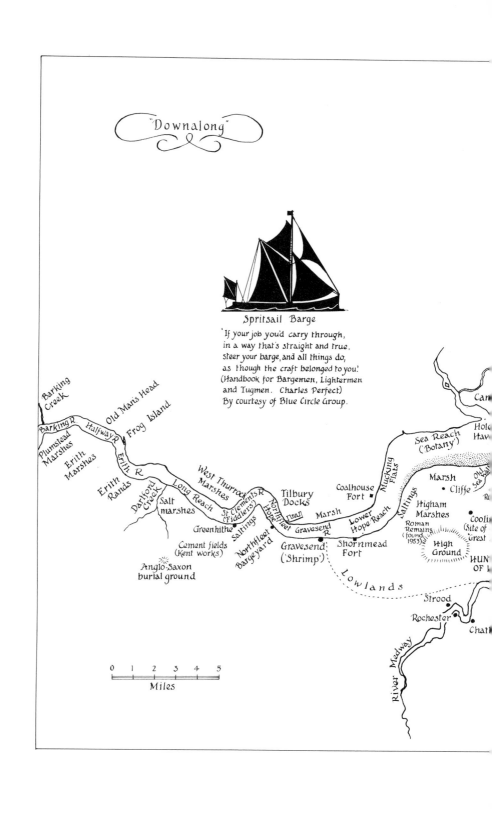

"Downalong"

Spritsail Barge

'If your job you'd carry through,
in a way that's straight and true,
steer your barge, and all things do,
as though the craft belonged to you.'
(Handbook for Bargemen, Lightermen
and Tugmen. Charles Perfect)
By courtesy of Blue Circle Group.

Barking Creek

Barking R

Plumstead Marshes

Erith Marshes

Halfway R

Old Mans Head

Frog Island

Erith R

Erith Rands

Dartford Creek

Long Reach

Salt marshes

West Thurrock Marshes

St Clements R

Greenhithe

Saltings

Cement fields (Kent works)

Anglo-Saxon burial ground

Northfleet Bargeyard

Northfleet Hope

Northfleet R

Tilbury Docks

Gravesend R

Marsh

Gravesend ('Shrimp')

Coalhouse Fort

Lower Hope Reach

Shornmead Fort

Mucking Flats

Sea Reach ('Botany')

Saltings

Marsh

• Cliffe

Higham Marshes

Roman Remains (found 1953)

High Ground

Lowlands

Hole

Hav

Cliffe

Cooli (Site of Great

HUN OF

Can

Strood

Rochester

Chat

River Medway

0 1 2 3 4 5
Miles

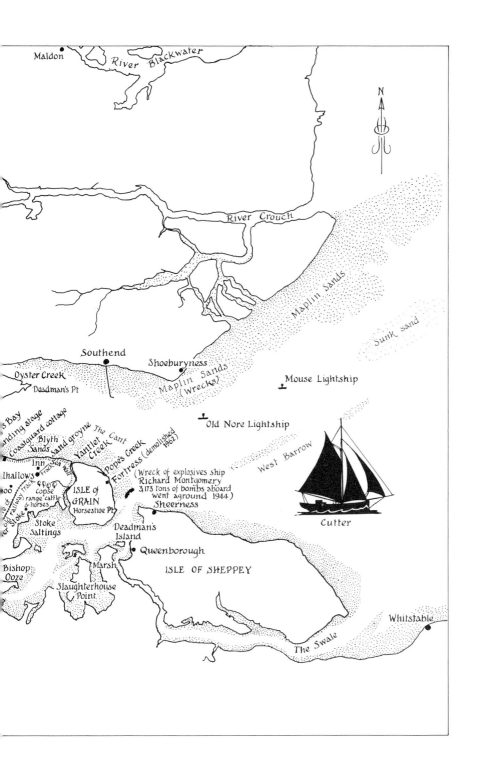

Maldon

River Blackwater

N

River Crouch

Maplin Sands

Sunk sand

Southend

Shoeburyness

Oyster Creek

Deadman's Pt

Maplin Sands
(Wrecks)

Mouse Lightship

's Bay

anding stage

Coastguard cottage

Blyth
Sands   sand groyne   The Cant

Yantlet Creek

Inn   'n Sea

lhallows

copse

range cattle
& horses

ISLE of
GRAIN
Horseshoe Pt

Popes Creek

Fortress (demolished 1962)

Old Nore Lightship

West Barrow

(Wreck of explosives ship
Richard Montgomery
3,173 tons of bombs aboard
went aground 1944)
Sheerness

Stoke
Saltings

Deadman's
Island

Bishop
Ooze

Marsh

Queenborough

ISLE OF SHEPPEY

Slaughterhouse
Point

Sharp

Whitstable

The Swale

Cutter

retaining the characteristics of its medieval forerunner. In its crudest form it was still simply a floating shallow box, its bows blunt with a sheer bow or 'swim'. Known as a dumb barge or blind barge by sailormen, it was a hazardous vessel to get too close to in a small dinghy. For if the current was strong enough, the rower could be sucked under the lighter's overhang and down under its keel.

Although many sailormen were also fully licensed lightermen and watermen, the demarcation between the two jobs remained. The latter could carry passengers, the former freight only, and it was an expensive game for a lighterman to attempt to take a fare.

Thames watermen in the Pool of London near the Tower, 1890s.

One hangover from the days when the Thames had been the waterman and lighterman's sole domain was the freewater clause which survives today, provided no engine has been installed in the barge or lighter. While the dock keepers and dock gate controllers, known as bogeymen, were screwing the last penny out of shipping companies on behalf of the dock owners, the sailing lightermen plied free, for the freewater clause allowed for 'no charge for lighters or craft entering docks to convey, deliver or receive ballast or goods to and from on board any ship'.

By it a lighterman working under sail could simply – or not so simply, as fights often ensued – enter a dock, tie up his lighter on the offside of a vessel and offload from there, saving his employer the expense of dockers' fees. Shipping companies were quick to spot this dodge, and simply anchored in the Pool, and awaited the fleet of lighters which would save them untold brass in exorbitant wharfside docking. With the advent of the ungainly looking steam paddle tug, things got even more convenient. A tug skipper or 'Tosher' (who was probably a registered waterman anyway) could tow a long string of lighters to a ship, drop his 'villick' (anchor) alongside, and watch the lightermen leaping around like agile gazelles, throwing ropes and hawzers as if they were featherweights, and unload in half the time. This was a mixed blessing to the older lightermen who viewed the steam tugs with derision. 'Bah – a wooden post would make a lighterman these days!'

Harry Thomas Harris, a Southwark lighterman, was ·born in 1880, a sixth generation waterman going back to George Harris in 1685, and he is especially interesting because he went to the trouble of keeping notebooks in which he recorded details of the waterman's life at the turn of the century. He was apprenticed in 1894 at twelve shillings a week in the year of the opening of Tower Bridge, when one of the last great water processions with state barges was seen. Along with his father, he rowed his lighter upriver in the pageant, using the wide twenty-four foot sweeps which the modern apprentice still has to master. (A good lighterman could drive a fully loaded lighter as much as fifteen miles with one sweep, by taking advantage

Opening of Tower Bridge, 1894.

of the current – many can still do this in competition.) At Tower Bridge they were boarded by sightseers. 'I can still feel the itch in my hand to pick up the sixpences and coppers from the thwart, also the sinking feeling as Father frowned and gave a negative nod.' As lightermen, of course, they were not licensed to take fares.

Lighterman Harry Thomas Harris, left, with Bill, Charlotte (Lottie) and Harry in Sunday best on a rare excursion to Ramsgate.

Harry Thomas Harris got his licence in 1896 and was at first allowed charge of punts, loading glass for Nine Elms. Nowadays each lighter bears a registered name and official number and tonnage. The owner's number, registered with the Port of London Authority, is usually marked on the 'huddis' or stern, sometimes with an emblem such as a Maltese Cross or the Blue Circle of the cement companies.

The upriver lightermen belonged to a tight-knit community – often tracing their ancestry back to the most distant recorded time, and within the community, families are still known by early nicknames: the Robinsons are 'Cockies' still; the Blyths 'Nellies'; the Hopkins 'Pollys'; and the Marshes are variously 'Stackys', 'Stiffys', 'Rum' or 'Regs'. The traditional lighterman was a colourful figure on the river, usually in a shiny black stove hat, and dressed in collar and necktie – even into the 1950s it was not unknown for lightermen to be dressed in bowler hats and waistcoated suit. If a dirty job came along, the lighterman would simply strip down to his 'shreddies' and dress himself to the nines when the job was done. Boots, too, stamped a man's locality, according to Harry Thomas Harris: "Boots were pegged or sewn; a glance at a man's boots would tell who was the maker – every riverside district had its shoemaker – this causing heated arguments as to the merits of each."

If the wind was in the wrong direction and whipped away a man's voice before he could tell the old woman on shore that he would not be home for dinner, a whole range of arm signals would suffice. After he had given his neighbourhood's whistle and kin ashore could look up to see him pass, a wave from the elbow followed by a long one from the shoulder indicated that the lighterman was bound 'downalong' or the lower reaches, a wave crosswise above the head symbolised 'upalong' and probably home that night for a visit, in Harris's case to Fatties Music Hall – favourite haunt of watermen where a fraternity song was:

> Sing up for fatties,
> Cheer up for fatties,
> Why make life a load.
> Sing up for fatties,
> You know where that is –
> Down in the Westminster Bridge Road.

In river slang, a long night's work was called a 'Tidgin' or 'Dukla' and signified 'pack a bag'; a 'thgin' was an early night, and these phrases would not be unfamiliar to a modern lighterman still hoping for a job which would be a 'full roadun' – a full week's work.

The strength of these men was renowned, gained from a lifetime spent manhandling a squat loaded lighter with nothing but two twenty-eight feet 'sweeps' and their own muscle power. Many were fine boxers, and had their own ring at Blackfriars, and Bankside characters going by the robust names of Podge, Willow-Eye, Wiggy, Titchy (who was 6′ 2″) Mad Brady, Moaner, Whisper Rivers, and 'Wooden Heights' who supplied coal by lighter and whose speciality was swinging heavy sacks of the stuff as if they were bags of feathers. One day he excelled himself, the combined weight of 'Wooden Heights' and the coal broke clear through the bottom of his boat and sank in full view of friends and relations who never let him forget it.

Through Harry Thomas Harris's notes, we get an interesting picture of the younger generation versus the 'old bear', the pre-steam lighterman, to whom he was bound as a boy, and with it, a peek at the skills which an apprentice has to master to this day:

> Being sent to Fresh Wharf to assist an old Bear (Old Bonsor) with a barge downriver to London Dock Shadwell, I said, "Good morning, Mr. Corpos."
>
> He gave me one glance, growling, "What do ye want?"
>
> I, answering in the river parlance, replied "I'm your mate!"
>
> Contempt for my far from robust figure brought the question: "Does your schoolmaster know you're not at school today?"
>
> "Yes, thank you," I said.
>
> The soft answer did not turn away wrath; he told me never to be saucy to my elders. We started our journey down, I anxious to make a good impression. "Take your oar aft" was the first order. The operation looks simple but can only be performed by the initiated. The handle is grasped in one hand, with the other hand canting the blade with a turn of the wrist causing the blade to plane away from the barge's side; if this canting was not done the oar would come parallel to the gunwhale, the handle beyond one's reach, and either the oar had to be released or into the 'ditch' you would go with the oar.
>
> Now I was taught this when a schoolboy taking rides with my father, and as I had already had two years' strenuous training with him I could handle and balance an oar with the next. Running along the narrow gunwhale with the oar as far as the 'quarter' I choose the point of balance and with a quick weigh down of the handle threw the oar into its working position against the stern post, in less time than these words were penned. In this position the barge is steered, and being helped ahead and slightly sideways if desired.
>
> I was soon in unison with the navigation down, anticipating orders while threading through the numerous channels left us by the large number of sailing barges at anchor at Shadwell. Actually, Old Bonsor hardly gave an order, I was already doing it.
>
> I knew, that he knew, that I knew! After this day my reception with him was much more cordial!

Old London Bridge, when Harris' grandfather recalled nervous fares leaping out to rejoin their passage beyond its perilous arches, had gone by this time, but even today it is dangerous to under-estimate the twisting currents that stream under any of the river arches. Even with the power of heavy-duty engines, in Harris's day, it was a manoeuvre calling for extreme dexterity.

There was Westminster Bridge "with its buttress edges like knives, like a ship's ram", and 'Upalong' lightermen were very contemptuous of the efforts of the below bridge man.

Apart from navigational hazards, a bridge could raise a domestic danger, too, if you believed a riverside superstition going right up to the 1940s. Crossing the water too many times on romantic missions produced the caution:

> If when you court 'er
> She lives over the water,
> Twins it'll be –
> Just you see!

The usual working of a craft above bridge if double-handed, was to send the junior aft to steer and at the same time by laying the oar well round the stem help the headway. The advantage of this was every bridge with numerous arches was built on a bend of the river such as Waterloo, Vauxhall, Battersea, Barnes and Kew; here the tide would set away from the point; by slightly steering at an angle when shaping for the 'bridge hole' as the arch was called, the hand aft rowing against the man forward, a barge could be edged up against the set as well as increasing the headway . . . just before entering the hole, the barge was straightened up and the bridge shot . . . After shooting Vauxhall on a strong spring tide, the barge would gather enough headway to shoot her into the wharf about a mile above without too much effort.

The spring tides left many parts of the shore exposed at low water, and at this time lighters would be wharfed and bucket loads of hard core were raked over and then topped off with Kentish chalk from a 'Chalkie' sailing barge. All this paddling around in the muck was designed to create a barge 'hard' 'where an old lady could settle her bottom snug', and at inlets such as Jennings Wharf and Sun Wharf where such a hard existed, there could be seen each spring tide a man doing his 'King Canute' act as he swept the muddy water. This was the job of the original 'mudlark' or 'luter' – incidentally, just at this point, beneath all the bicycle wheels and Pepsi cans, is the discarded masonry of old London Bridge if the enthusiast cares to dig deep enough.

Another vanished profession above bridge, was the 'huffler' from the Dutch word 'hoveller': the name became split with several meanings – downriver it meant a river pilot, particularly in Essex and Kent, but upriver, his special job was to help lower the sail and mast sometimes in split seconds, as the barge shot through the arches. In Harris's time, one of the most well-known seems to have been Tom Cunis, whose family are still lightering. Characterised by his small 'dish' with which he sculled over to each client, he seems to have been somewhat verbose on the latest activities of his passion, the Old Vic run by the bespectacled eccentric, Lilian Baylis (who possessed a vocabulary as colourful as any of her Banksiders), and one can imagine the frustration as the 'hole' loomed up perilously close, whilst Tom Cunis rattled on about the finer points of 'The Bohemian Girl' down the Waterloo Road.

Out in all weathers, lightermen were used to wind and rain but they hated ice and fog. Harris wrote: "I have seen a fish-cutter bound for Billingsgate below Tower Bridge. Then high water came – the bridge opened but the vessel was unable to move – it was a solid block of ice . . . It was peculiar how the ice disappeared when the thaw came with rain . . . the lightermen, however, cared little how it had quickly vanished, all being anxious to see the end of this period."

Fog appeared with regular monotony, and when one pictures the congestion on the river, and the bargemen equipped only with a whistle, or in some cases a drum, it's amazing how they managed to stay clear of 'sidewinders', a scrape, or if very unlucky a 'gutser' which could send a man to the bottom when very few of them could swim.

At the onset of a 'particular' (a really bad pea-souper) "the lighterman might carry on and be lucky if he finishes the job, the ears becoming eyes, and all senses alert to get a bearing, yelling out to anchored craft 'Where are you?' – sometimes, a smart 'You ought to be locked up being under way in this weather.' "

Some of the anchored craft would probably have been small waterborne retailers. A mop over the stern signified a rope-seller. A pail, a water-seller. A coalsack hoisted from a mast, a coal-seller or in some cases a 'dredger', for many lightermen earned a supplementary income in hard times by dredging coal dropped from colliers at Beckton. A fast-moving galley with obligingly conspicuous white-tipped oars would warn of a police-boat from 'suicide centre' as the police wharf was known. Whether the police (or 'oglers' in river parlance) ever twigged about this early warning system is unknown.

Pilfering was rife, and whilst the law-abiding lighterman might confine himself to trapping pigeons to supplement the evening meal, the technique of tapping off liquor from barrels was a common practice. "'Do it clean' was the maxim. This was accomplished by gently tapping the hoops of the barrel towards the thinner end and then boring two small holes. After the 'waxer' had been drawn, the holes were neatly bunged and the hoops hammered back."

Small wonder, however, as metal lighters replaced wood, the relationship between lightermen and sailormen was a tenuous alliance. The destructive bows of the new craft were a source of constant fear to the sailorman and his woodwork.

Apparently the smell of liquor turned Harry Harris off, but "I must confess that I never refused a tin of pines or similar goods." That many lightermen took more than one waxer is clear from a trip Harris took from Victoria Dock with seventy tons of wheat for French's Mill at Bow Bridge, which meant manoeuvring a large lighter up the River Lea, or Bow Creek. He was fifteen or sixteen years old at the time and obliged to manoeuvre the heavily laden craft single-handed for four hours while his guvnor slept off his excesses in the cabin below.

The opportunity for sleep seemed to be a hit and miss affair with apprenticed boys. In the case of any job with 'Big Nibby' it was impossible.

> He was a mountain of flesh – fat everywhere, which made the eyes appear small; he was very nimble of foot considering his bulk . . . Having acquired the knack of sleeping standing up, he would have several naps on the journey, holding the handle of the oar, blade swaying and rocking to the swell . . . When going to sleep in the cabin, he would not, perhaps he could not, lie down, sitting wedged facing the fire, he would sway sideways, but then surge forward just missing the fire. At this point, snorts and gurgles would be emitted, the performance being repeated the whole time that he was in the cabin. If the lad could find a 'better 'ole' he took the opportunity. Some would rather face the cold than those porcine snorts.

However, the majority of lightermen were wide-awake, hard working and scrupulously honest, in many cases handling large sums of money on behalf of their employers, and meticulously accounting for each of the farthings that they so easily could have fiddled.

Harry Thomas Harris again:

The watermen and lightermen of my youth were proud of their river knowledge. Credit was always given to a skilful man; to be judged by your peers and given the verdict, 'He's a good lighterman' was gratifying to one who had made their work a pride. If one earned this epithet, it was known among the fraternity with the result that employment could be in a sense, chosen. I believe that the critical eye of those parents, uncles, cousins, neighbours, was a big incentive to these lads to whole-heartedly work and learn everything possible required to make them 'shape like a lighterman'. As a class they were loyal to each other, jealous of 'the privilege' (Freedom of the River), clannish as the Clans, mildly tolerant of landsmen, benevolent to anyone in trouble.

Licensed uniformed waterman in single seater ferry 1890's.

Greenwich waterman 1750. Still wearing the loose tubular breeches popular 100 years before.

6

The Chain Gang

You'll enjoy a quiet crust
More by rubbing off the dust.
It's a maxim that should never be forgot.
Whilst labour leads to wealth,
And will keep you in good health
So its best to be contented with your lot.
Work boys work and be contented
As long as you've enough to buy a meal,
The man you may rely
Will be wealthy by and by
If you'll only keep your shoulders to the wheel.

'Work Boys Work' –
Cole Hole Tavern

IN 1801 THE POPULATION of London was less than a million. By the 1890s the docks had spread from St. Katharine's, by Tower Bridge in the west, round the loop of Millwall, and east to the Royal Victoria and the Royal Albert across the water from Woolwich, and the population of the capital was over three million, with the dockers clustered in the crowded tenements of Stepney, Poplar and Canning Town. For a visiting artist like Gustave Doré "London had nothing more picturesque nor striking to show than the phases of her river and her boundless docks. And hereabouts we tarried week after week, never wearying of the rich variety of form, colour and incident." In 1870 the Thames was still the obvious core and heart of the city to draw visitors to it, and Doré has left us a stunning collection of drawings. His pictures capture the costume of the London docker, and his exaggerated elongation of thin bodies and drawn faces, the grind of the work which, except for a few professional dockers, stamped the poor wretches who turned to 'humping' as a last resort. It is, however, still the illustration of an outsider.

Dock workers by Doré.

The Victorian chronicler, Mayhew, also wandered inquisitively through dockland, notebook in hand, capturing the sights and smells:

> Along the quay you see now men with their faces blue with indigo, and now gaugers with their long brass-tipped rule dripping with spirit from the cask they had been probing. Then will come a group of flaxen haired sailors chattering German; and next a black sailor, with a cotton handkerchief twisted turban-like round his head. Presently a blue-smocked butcher with fresh meat and a bunch of cabbages in the tray on his shoulder, and shortly afterwards a mate with green paraquets in a cage. Here you will see a sorrowful-looking woman, with bright new cooking tins at her feet, telling you she is a emigrant preparing for her voyage. As you pass along the quay the air is pungent with tobacco; or that it overpowers you with the fumes of rum; then you are nearly sicked with the stench of hides and huge bins of horns; and shortly afterwards, the atmosphere is fragrant with coffee and spice . . . the fumes of wines, and there, the peculiar fungus smell of dry-rot – there the jumble of sounds as you pass along the dock blends in anything but sweet concord. The sailors are singing boisterous nigger songs from the Yankee ships just entering; the cooper is hammering at the casks on the quay; the chains of cranes loosed of all their weight rattle as they fly up again. The ropes splash in the water; some captain shouts his orders through his hands; a goat bleats from some ship in the basin; and empty casks roll along the stones with a heavy drum-like sound.

Romantic the docks certainly were on the face of it, and a good living could be had for the skilled man and his family, but to the majority, the catch-hand labourer, unskilled and undernourished, thinking himself lucky if he could go back home with a tanner in his pocket, the exciting smells and sights must have been a dismal mockery. The terrible conditions of the average casual docker persisted well into this century and one man was eloquent on the subject of labouring on the docks when he told Jack London in 1901: 'Garn! Wot's yor game eh? A missus kissin' and kids climbin', and the kettle singin? – all on four pounds ten shillings a month when you 'ave a ship, and four pound nuthin' when you 'aven't? I'll tell you wot I'd get fer four pounds ten shillings – a missus rowin', kids squallin', no coal to make the kettle sing, and the kettle up the spout, that's wot I'd get . . . Arf and Arf's good enough fer me!" Arf 'n Arf, was booze, and it's here that one of the accepted traditions started – the long-held belief that the waterfront signified booze, brawling and profanity. The decriers don't bother to delve deeper into the reasons why so many of these human packhorses soused themselves up to the eyebrows every Saturday night in a weekly attempt to lose themselves, and the word 'docker' is often still, quite wrongly, synonymous with a drunken brawler.

In fact, like all the waterfront trades, it had its hierarchy. At the bottom of the ladder, the labourers who made for the docks as a last resort in a frantic effort to keep themselves and their families out of the spike. At the top were the stevedores. London docks were unique in separating import and export dock labour. Stevedores had a monopoly of loading vessels (their name derives from the Spanish *estivar* – to stow) which demanded great skill in trimming a vessel to keep its balance, and great manual dexterity in confined spaces. The stevedores were an élite, not employed by the dock companies. The companies only unloaded vessels, a simpler process just requiring speed and strength. This is where the catch-hand casual came in, though skilled dockers, particularly at the Royal Albert and Victoria, could earn good wages on a more or less constant contract. The deal porters at the Surrey and Commercial possessed the balance of tightrope walkers as they casually marched up and down planks of wood high above the wharfside, balancing five or six thirty-foot sections of deal uncannily on shoulders that became as calloused and leathery as a saddle. While the guano men, who unloaded their mucky cargoes from sailing ships which had spent two years in the Pacific, could earn up to a sovereign a day.

One particularly arduous job which could more properly have been called 'coolie', was that of the 'coalie' or coal-heaver. In the days of steam when northern flat-irons or colliers were disgorging millions of tons of coal to fill Mayfair grates and monster power-stations, and where dozens of merchant and passenger liners had to be 'coaled', hundreds of men were employed in the backbreaking work of manhandling coal to and from lighters, and the sailing bargeman must have shaken his head and wondered if it was all worth the effort. Harry Thomas Harris, sweeping downriver, re-members the blackened faces of the 'humpers' who worked on right up to the age of the diesel engine:

> Just a little lower down on the Charlton side were the coal derricks, one or two. Coals were discharged then from ships moored here; if a soft coal was being unloaded, clouds of coaldust would be observed rising. A

passing tug running light to Victoria Dock would have a gang of coalies on her deck returning to shore having been relieved. They would be covered in dust, the lips showing red as cherries, the dust having been washed off by the application of the tea-bottle, the whites of the eyes also a contrast to the all black appearance. If near enough to us we would whistle, "Whist, here come the bogey-man!" but all coalies then appeared aged and repartee was not their strong point.

Coaling the Homeric.

Another dirty, and extremely dangerous job was that of the ships' painter, but if unpleasant it was at least plentiful. The work had always to be done at the gallop, time being money. The paint of the time was a highly inflammable and toxic mixture of meths, petroleum and benzine, which could sear a man's lungs or burst into sudden flame. The best safeguard was to work in a gang of three or four and to dispense with a light, but more often than not, a single man had to creep through a minute shaft and paint lying down so that he could not help inhaling noxious fumes which might kill him years on.

Work was divided into 'task' and 'contract', task being piece work at fivepence an hour and contract being for a pre-arranged sum or wage. If the ship was unloaded in less time than expected, the men were paid a proportion of the money saved, or 'plus', an insidious way to make men work harder, and greedily exploited by the companies. This 'sweating money' as it was known, was later divided between the Royals only. Sub-contracting was an even bigger door to graft and corruption, the contract filtering down through as many as seven contractors who received garnish all the way down. Finally there were 'agents' who gave out preference tickets in local pubs, which is another reason why so many humpers were obliged to hang around the pubs. Quite often a man was taken on before dinner and then signed off quickly to avoid meal fees. If he had had no breakfast in the first place, his chances of lasting out the day and qualifying for a 'plus' were minimal anyway.

Around London Docks were the real slums; it was here that the bloodiest brawls and most melancholy sights were to be seen. Here lived the 'casuals', laid-off bricklayers' labourers or field-workers who were dependent upon seasonal work, and turned to the docks when the weather closed in. Most of them had reached the bottom, and did not have either the physique or the diet to maintain the nine to ten hours work which was required of them. Many of them were without boots, so they bound their feet in rags, hence their nickname of 'Toe-rag'. Many came to work (if they were lucky enough to catch 'the eye') without having eaten a meal in twenty-four hours. Some managed to keep going to four o'clock, by which time sheer fatigue took over and they were simply unable to lift another thing, thus giving rise to the belief that dockers were a lazy lot. Occasionally pity took hold and a dock contractor would engage the poorer men for small jobs such as unloading figs or light cargoes, but since

A fight at the 'calling on' chain.

most of the choicer loads were the province of preference men and the demarcation lines rigorously enforced, this can't have happened often.

Amongst full-time dockies there existed an age-old suspicion of immigrant labour, and it was true that this vast army of catch-hand scarecrows did undercut the professional's bargaining ground.

At this time, parts of London had all the sectarian 'no-go' symptoms of the Ardoyne in Belfast today. Between London Bridge and Tower Bridge a narrow way known as Battle Bridge Lane leads from the Southern shore to Tooley Street. An L-shaped alley turns off the left hand side and joins it a little later on. In maps dated 1848 the alley was marked 'English Ground', and near it is a small hatched area 'Irish Ground' – it doesn't actually add the word 'only', but the inference is clear.

One of the biggest iniquities of the dock labour system was 'calling on'. By this system, men simply stood at the chain by the dock gate and hoped to 'catch the eye' of the contractor or ganger. At a hearing in 1888 a docker called James Gray described his experience of calling on to a select committee of the House of Lords on the sweating system:

As a rule I have to struggle for employment. Yesterday I earned two and threepence; this is the first work I have done since last Friday . . . I have been down at the London Docks, No. 5 gate every morning since last Friday, at the usual hour of calling on, that is, eight thirty a.m., and I have been unsuccessful in obtaining employment until yesterday; yesterday I was there from eight thirty till eleven thirty. At eleven thirty I should say that there was something like 350 men waiting for employment at this special gate. A contractor by the name of Clemence came to the gate, for I think it was, fourteen men; it was either fourteen or sixteen men; of course there was a struggle. As I said before, they have a certain number of tickets to give out; and there was a struggle between us men at the gate who should be lucky enough, as it were, to gain one of these tickets.

It is a common occurrence for men to get seriously injured in a struggle like that. Your Lordships may imagine a kind of cage, as it were, where men struggle like wild beasts; we stand upon one another's shoulders. I myself have had eight or ten men on my shoulders and my head, and I have been hurt several times in a struggle for employment like that, though I have been at the docks every morning at the usual time for calling on . . . the usual time I am fortunate enough to get employment is between eleven and one o'clock; that is to say, I have the privilege, it may be called, of earning from one and ninepence to two and sixpence . . .

Beyond the chain, men wait expectantly before the rush, 1903.

Ben Tillett, Secretary of the Dock Labourers' Union spoke at that same hearing, and estimated that there were 100,000 labourers on the docks, of which only 2,400 belonged to his union – the reason was clear.

It was a brave man who attempted to change things. Dan Cullen, a self-educated docker who had tried to improve the working conditions of the fruit porters in the late eighties had had to endure ten years of 'discipline' or 'drilling'. This meant being called on for the minimum two or three days a week which ensured him a starvation wage but no more. In this way his employers gave him just enough work to avoid trouble but not enough work for him to live on. Jack London records Cullen's one room in Leman Street behind all the riches of St. Katharine's dock. Just big enough to house a bed and a broken chair, the walls were covered with pictures of Garibaldi, Engels, John Burns and other labour leaders, together with hundreds of squashed bugs. "Each mark a violent death." This broken man, who loved the Old Vic and Shakespeare, was carried by a docker friend to the Temperance Hospital and died there a pauper patient, of Brights' Disease and dropsy, in 1900.

The docks were rife with strikes, the most notable being the dockers' tanner strike of 1889 when the contract system was abolished and piece work substituted at sixpence per hour. Ben Tillet marched at the head of an army of dockers, behind him the brass band of the stevedores, lightermen, ships' painters, deep-sea sailors, fishermen, riggers, engineers and shipwrights. "Permanent men got up respectably, preferables got up to look like permanents, and unmistakable casuals with vari-coloured patches on their faded greenish garments." With them marched watermen, some in their ceremonial scarlet coats, pink stockings and pewter badges resplendent on their arms, incongruous next to the coalies who travelled in wagons with leather bags suspended on long poles with which they cajoled coppers from the watching crowds. A long procession of floats followed them. Watermen's wherries on wheels, models of Neptune fashioned by the womenfolk, more sombre effigies of starving dockies' children, contrasting tableaux representing the sweater's dinner and the docker's dinner . . .

Scab labour was brought in but did not survive for long in the face of such a unified front. Eventually the companies paid direct, and the Royals' monopoly of plus payments was opened out to everybody, but calling on remained, and there was still no compensation to a dock labourer for injuries received at work. Very few men were supplied with suitable clothing for the foul weather they sometimes had to work in or the filthy cargoes they had to handle. Still, the strike got its dockers their tanner an hour and the populace breathed again.

The calling on system was not abolished until 1965, after the findings of the Devlin Committee on the Port Transport Industry. This also abolished piece work, and established a regular working wage and security of employment for registered dockers.

Licensed porter, St. Katharine's Dock, 1870's.

7

Mudlarks

There is some folks wot takes it meek,
And starves theirselves to 'scape the beak,
While us 'deluded' kids are slick – as Bottomuppermosts.

MUDLARKS VARIED IN degree from the youngest filching in the mud
for useful pickings, to organised gangs which put Fagin in the shade.
When one considers that the wife of a casual docker could usually
earn more than her husband by taking in washing, and that rarely
covered the daily grocery bill, one realises that the mudlarks were
essential to augment a meagre income. Many of them were coal-
humpers' children, Dad having accidentally dropped the odd lump
for his son or daughter to filch later, and this fairly innocuous
practice often formed a boy's apprenticeship to bigger things.
Actually to climb on a barge and steal coal was a very serious affair.
Filching collected a swipe round the ear, stealing from a vessel could
collect three weeks to a month in prison, age notwithstanding. This
was the Londoner's adaptation of the country boy's 'scrumping'; if
the apple was a windfall you were in the clear, if it was plucked from
the tree you were in for it. English literature is liberally sprinkled
with cosy stories of mudlarks as if they were playing naughty pranks
instead of fighting a desperate game for survival. After a look at their
conditions we can perhaps appreciate the ex-mudlarks Billy Smith
and Charlie Eaton who, finding a genuine medallion on the Thames,
turned to forging artifacts which are still fooling antique buffs.

Mayhew found it impossible to gauge just how many children
were involved in mudlarking; certainly it was common practice

Mudlarks.

among all waterfront children. It was an age-old tradition for barge-men and lightermen to dredge for coal droppings on slack days, and the river was, and still is, a combing ground for kids of all ages. A large army of children, mostly between the ages of eight to fourteen used regularly to scavenge closely circumscribed areas, and the famous story immortalised on film and television of one such youngster who scavenged up one particularly hallowed sewer outlet and caused a national sensation by coming up in the region of a royal palace, causing untold panic amongst the Queen's Guard, is based on truth. However the whole era of the mudlark has become bogged down in a veritable treacle-pudding of sentiment, which slides happily over the awful realities. Let one boy speak for himself, though I suspect Mayhew corrected his grammar here and there:

> I was born in London – my family were all born in Ireland. My father works at London Docks. He is a strong-bodied man of thirty-four. I was sent to school with my brothers for about three years, and learned reading and writing and arithmetic. One of my brothers has been at sea for five years. I work . . . in the neighbourhood of Millwall picking up

pieces of coal and iron, copper and bits of canvas on the surface. When bargemen heave coal to be carried from the shore . . . some of it falls in the mud and we afterwards pick it up . . . the most I ever saw my companions find was one shilling's worth a day.

There are generally thirteen or fourteen mudlarks, boys and girls, around Limehouse in the summer and six boys steadily in the winter . . . They are generally good swimmers. When a bargeman gets hold of one, he generally throws them overboard when they swim inshore and dry their clothes . . . I have been chased twice by the police galley.

The fraternity was a tight one and had many allies ashore. The same boy describes bolting himself under the hatch of a moored barge whilst the police tried to break the lock. Unsuccessful, they had sculled over to his clothes in an attempt to take them and force him out, but an accomplice had seen the ploy and hidden them.

Read between the lines of another of Mayhew's testaments, and imagine the desperation which prompted one mudlark to swim underwater in putrid and noxious filth, at night, in winter, and in imminent danger of being crushed between dock gates.

One night I saw at Young's Dock a large piece of copper drop down where a vessel was being repaired . . . That evening as a ship was coming out of the docks, I stripped off my clothes and dived down several feet, seized the piece of copper and carried it away, swimming by the side of the vessel. As it was dark I was not observed by any of the crew nor by any of the men who opened the dock gates. I fetched it ashore and sold it to a marine dealer.

The most he would have got would have been a penny-half-penny for a pound of copper at a time when ten shillings would buy a room for the week, and bread for a family of five for six days, or it would buy a yard of silk for a bonnet – it depends on your point of view . . .

With, by the mid 1800s, some 8,000 vessels in the four miles below London Bridge, and some 2,000 above, as *The Times* reported in 1867, together with 163 known receivers in the metropolitan area of central London alone, the temptation for a mudlark to move up or – whichever way you choose to look at it – down, the ladder, were endless, and just as the legitimate riverside trades had their specialists, so did the illegitimate, including quite an army of chameleons who were pure as the driven snow by day and 'on the fiddle' by night:

In Arundel Street the lawyers abound.
At the foot of the street, the barges are found.
Fly! Honesty – fly to some safer retreat,
For there's craft in the river, and craft in the street.
Why should Honesty seek any safer abode
Than with lawyers and barges, Odd rot 'em,
For the lawyers are just at the top of the road,
And the barges are just at the bottom!

The real hangouts were the docks themselves. With all the wealth daily handled by some of the poorest labourers in London it was bound to attract sticky fingers despite stringent overseeing by dock police, some of whom were fairly 'game' themselves.

Not helping any to improve the bad reputation which the casual labourer had, was the 'scuffle-hunter' who got himself signed on for a day's work wearing an overlong apron liberally supplied with capacious pockets into which small pieces could be thrust when the ganger wasn't looking – this might have been our mudlark a few years on. The scuffle-hunting dodge was short-lived however, because by more stringent laws, he was not allowed ashore during the day, and no baggy trousers, bags or aprons were allowed at the work site. A system of body search was also likely to be called without warning. Many mudlarks were actively in league with lumpers – probably relations who were adroit at slinging bags of stolen cargo over a vessel's sides for a mudlark to retrieve, especially round the gas works' coal barges, Waterloo Bridge and St. Paul's Wharf.

Then there were numerous essential jobs which enabled a fellow to insinuate himself inside the docks. Rat-catching (often with trained pet rats which could be introduced to a vessel, captured, and used again) and garbage collecting both offered the chance for a boy to get himself some 'translators' at the least; that is, to swipe a crewman's washing off a line, for highest prices were paid for translatable boots or 'gallies'. Then there was the 'Betty' or lightning picklock. If he was adept enough, he might be recruited into a regular gang with a linking chain reaching right down to a hangout or 'ken' around King David Lane in Shadwell, noted for its receivers of stolen tobacco, or Elephant Stairs at Rotherhithe, where anything lifted was rarely seen again, the area being a maze of passages, or 'Rat's Castle' in St. Giles, whence a certain Inspector Field had sent at least one member of every single family to New South Wales by the 1850s. The night plunderers, as they were known, might pass themselves off as casuals by day, but would return at night in highly organised gangs equipped with black leather bags known as 'black straps' in which sugar or tea could be hived off a cask which had been marked during the day. Some mudlarks who were excellent swimmers would be recruited for towing over inflated bladders for tobacco or tea. More valuable cargoes were unloaded under the eye of a customs officer, and even some of these men were 'game' to look in the opposite direction if the price was right.

Above bridge, the pickings were mostly portable enough for a man to secrete on his person, but on the river itself, felonies were on a much larger scale, and often violent, from the 'sweepers', perhaps mudlarks who had acquired a boat, 'sweeping' up and down the tiers of moored vessels looking for the chance to lift anything that wasn't tied down, to the organised gangs, the Tier Rangers and River Pirates. Those called 'light-horsemen' operated by day. 'Light' presumably meant that they didn't actually hit anybody over the head in order to steal, but preferred to take advantage of the carrot-cruncher's fatigue after navigating up river. They'd cut loose his mooring lines (which carried a penalty of seven years' transportation), and follow at a discreet distance till the vessel ground into one of the many concealed inlets where they could pile aboard and help themselves. By night came the 'heavy horsemen'. More numerous, in some cases armed, they were not averse to laying out any kind of opposition including the police. They lowered a vessel's cargo into waiting boats – sometimes rowed by licensed watermen – and it took a small army to stop them. Some lightermen openly pinched their mates' vessels; the brothers Turnbull in 1858 helped themselves to two barges at Wapping containing lac dye and cases of wire whilst their crews were ashore. They took the barges over to Elephant Stairs where they were met by a carter, and once again, the goods disappeared into the receiver's backyard. Tom and Charlie Turnbull were not, however, so fortunate, and each got eighteen months' hard labour, and probably a lifetime's ostracism from the watermen's fraternity whose good standing they had threatened. Mayhew records the river pirates' main hang-outs as being Paddy's Goose Tavern in the Ratcliffe Highway, the dingier passages around Wapping and Bermondsey Wall, St. George's, Bluegate Fields, the Borough, and Dust Hole at Woolwich, although as the police became more adept at seeking them out and their 'kens' were 'coopered' or cover blown, they were constantly on the move.

In the main most people were surprisingly honest. When one recalls the sheer struggle and humiliation which a man went through in order to earn his honest tanner on the docks, the proportion of delinquents is small. Obviously, however, the crime wave could not have been successful without the connivance of some very skilled watermen. A landsman could never navigate the crowded tiers of shipping with lights dowsed, then make a landfall at a precise pin-spot at a precise time, nor understand the procedures in the dock, the intricacies of tide and time, or insinuate themselves into lucrative areas. But when one considers the prices paid for stolen goods – five 'finnies' (twenty-five pounds) for a bale of wire, three-halfpence a pound for old copper, a halfpenny a pound for canvas, a lifted pair of trousers or a jacket for fourpence at the dolly shop, all for a few hours' work – what price the docker's tanner?

Hot potato seller, Southwark, 1895.

The Old Gel

It was so old a ship – who knows, who knows?
– And yet so beautiful, I watched in vain
To see the mast burst open with a rose,
And the whole deck put on its leaves again.

J. Elroy Flecker

IF THE READER wants to grasp some of the beauty which lit up the sailormen's eyes as I listened to them talk of their 'old gels', you have to put on some wellies and stand in the mud off Yantlet Creek in the hope of seeing *Cambria* or *Cabby* round the Isle of Grain under full sail, and you'll be watching two of the few Thames sailing barges left performing much as nature intended. But the vessel as we know it today started in the Royal Navy, probably thanks to Pepys, looking out at the commercial barge-roads from his house in Greenwich. As well as a ship to shore loading vessel, which has culminated in the modern landing craft, the sailing barge was the decorated flag officer's barge which became, at its finest, the state barge. When the river was the natural focus for London ceremonial and spectacle, all the livery companies had their own state barges, the Lord Mayor's Show was celebrated with river, not road, processions until 1856 and foreign dignitaries worthy of a state welcome made their entry to the capital by river, rowed by teams of liveried watermen in barges bright with gold crustings and enormous flags. Perhaps the last time we saw but a shadow of this river ceremonial was in the funeral of Sir Winston Churchill.

In its workaday guise, however, the barge was a utility vessel, with nothing added unless to improve her handling capability and

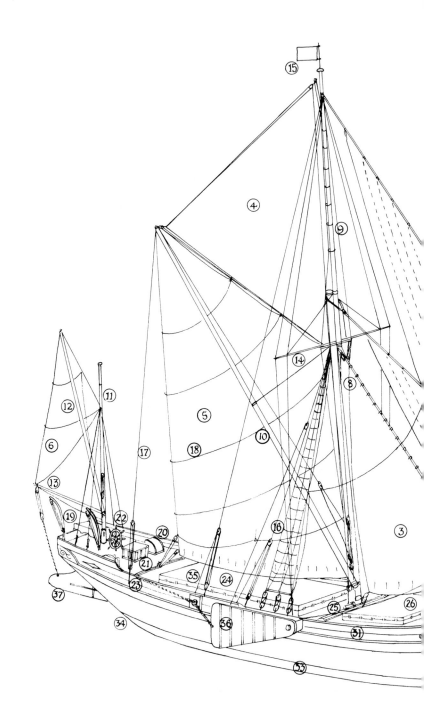

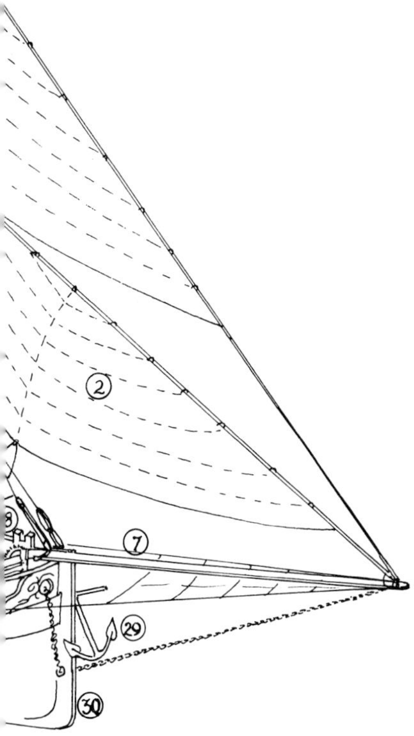

1 Staysail / Jib Topsail
2 Jib
3 Foresail
4 Topsail
5 Mainsail
6 Mizzen
7 Bowsprit
8 Mainmast
9 Top mast
10 Sprit
11 Mizzen mast
12 Mizzen sprit
13 Mizzen boom
14 Cross trees
15 Bob
16 Main runners
17 Wang
18 Main brail
19 Davits
20 Cuddy scuttle hatch
21 Cuddy skylight
22 Wheel
23 Main horse
24 Main hatch
25 Fore horse
26 Fore hatch
27 Fo'c'sle hatch
28 Windlass
29 Anchor ("Villick")
30 Stem
31 Rails
32 Wale
33 Chine
34 Run
35 Coamings
36 Leeboard
37 Rudder

Thames barge Cambria *under sail.*

the volume of her load. She was flat bottomed so she could operate close in-shore in shoal water, and remain upright when grounded. Her rigging evolved to keep down the cost of extra hands, and her unique hull took shape in order that she might navigate any kind of water from the Atlantic Ocean to a shallow inland creek – a sailor-man will joke, that if there's been a heavy dew the night before, his barge will float on it, and there's at least one story told of the mate who fell overboard whilst straining to raise the leeboard off Shoe-buryness, and literally ran after the barge which was blithely sailing on. Yet, formed as a purely practical animal, all those objective ingredients still combine to make a vessel of extraordinary beauty which cannot really be appreciated above bridge where she's rather like a fat old lady stripped down to a bikini, nor when she's chugging up an estuary with auxiliary engine, because of course it is her sails which top the picture.

Most of the pure wooden vessels were built to serve the demands of that great era of the Thames sailing barge from 1840 to 1928. There was a time when practically every little inlet with a convenient oak wood nearby had its builders' yard, earlier typified by Constable in his East Anglian sketches. There was Everards', Keep, Gold-smiths', Millers' of Deptford, Shrubshalls' at Ipswich (with another thirteen barges built at Limehouse), Piper's of Greenwich, Welling-ton Wharf at Lambeth, Southwark, Hutsons' of Maidstone, Short Brothers of Rochester, the Whites of Sittingbourne, the Pauls of Ipswich, the Horlocks and dozens of others. The job would take four men about three months to complete, and at the turn of the century, the price was one pound per ton capacity, so that a 110 tonner would bring in quite a few smokes at twopence for ten.

A barge-builder of the time would be fairly dismissive of the academic approach of boatbuilders now, for he probably wouldn't have recognised a blueprint if he saw one. His skill lay in his eye, and his drawing board was his imagination. It was a skill handed down, rather like the sailorman's handling of the craft being built, by word of mouth, generation to generation, and the builder's thumbnail was his slide-rule. Sometimes the most intricate little half inch scale models were built and these abound in maritime museums. From that the foreman, without batting an eyelid, would start hacking the huge keelson from a single elm tree which was laid out on the ground a few yards from the shoreline where it would blossom and shape to slip into the water a few months later. The backbone or keelson was shaped by hand tools in the saw-pit with two men push-ing and pulling, and with the ancient adze which is shaped rather like a hoe. The front of the keelson, or stem, would be fashioned to the individual builder's taste, some sharp, some bowed, and therefore no two barges are exactly alike. Then would come giant ribs of Oregon pine or English oak to support the huge weight of cargo. These were so flexible that laden barges have been known to beach themselves on rough ground and bend to such an extent that they resembled a humped-back bridge, and slide off with the tide, still watertight. The hull would be covered over with English oak and usually painted black. Whilst the vessel was solely intended as a workhorse, many barges possessed beautifully carved scrollwork on the stern and transom as a form of artist's signature. Perhaps there would be a double carved arrow, from Shrubshalls' yard, or inter-leaved ivy. All the barges built by the Howards were particularly decorative, having been carved, it is said, by the youngest son who was a cripple and therefore unable to do the heavier work. The acorn motif was very common in fiddle heads and transom decoration as a charm for fair weather, the acorn being a symbol of Thor, Norse god of Thunder.

Because a barge might have only three inches above the waterline, it was especially important that the deck planking was made completely watertight by wadding a mixture of tar and cow-hair between the planks and pressing them tightly together. The deck was invariably painted grey and treated to prevent slipping, and the gunwhales which ran like a rim round the vessel were usually white, again not for decoration but to give the skipper a clear idea of trim and level when loading – a bargeman's adaptation of the Plimsoll line.

The early barges were very similar in shape to the lighter, with a square sail like a Viking longship, but as their potential was realised, the blunt 'swim head' rather like that of a landing craft and diagonally shaped 'budget', gave way to the round bow and the 'transom' which gives the stern a champagne glass shape from which the rudder protruded. Around the turn of the nineteenth century when pilfering was rife, the open barge was closed in by decks and hatches known as 'dominoes' so that the cargo could be shut away from sticky fingers. The lee-board, which characterised her, had been adapted from the Dutch who taught us so much else in land reclamation and sailing, and was adopted because, venturing out into the estuary by the seventeenth century, the barge, being a shallow, flat-bottomed vessel unlike the schooner or yacht with a long keel beneath, could not sail well to windward, and the lee-board was lowered to act as a keel to help bite into the water and correct her inclination to drift sideways, The lee-board was a hinged, fan-shaped 'paddle' about sixteen feet long and seven feet wide at its broadest end. Hung opposite the mainmast and held by chains or 'pennants', it looked rather like a folded wing when not in use. The lee-board has to be hauled up manually every time the vessel has wind astern or wants to turn round or tack which is surely the reason why every sailorman appears to have arms stretching to the knees.

When I finally found myself on the deck of a coastal barge, she was as neat as Grandma's best parlour – a place for everything and everything in its place, and, trying not to give the game away by appearing a complete ignoramus, I began to study all those bits and pieces which had the most businesslike look to them. Hovering over the water beyond the bows pointed the bowsprit (minus the superfluous decoration of a figure-head) which supported the bowsprit shrouds and secured the topmast and jib stays. Behind this, an iron monster of a windlass raised the anchor on about sixty fathoms of chain. (A fathom was six feet, that much I knew because Grandad had said he hoped I wouldn't grow to a fathom or I'd be four inches taller than him, and his five feet eight inches was tall for a sailorman.) The anchor, or 'villick' above bridge, weighed about six hundredweight. The dolly-winch with cruel-looking cogs or 'ruffles' was turned to lower the five tons of mainmast and rigging at back-breaking speed as a bridge was approached, and was the reason at least one finger would be crushed in a lifetime. On deck were also visible a forward hatch, a main hatch, a cabin skylight and a scuttle. Aft was the steering wheel which had replaced the old tiller of our Viking ancestors around 1910. Neat pyramids of ropes, or sheets, of bass, cotton and hemp lay ready to be run out at a moment's notice. Then up aft, a small mizzen mast or jigger had been added to help the vessel's steering. Suspended on davits was a small dinghy, always propelled by sculling with one oar over the stern in a figure-of-eight motion – "Only idiots pulled their stomach muscles rowing," I was told. But was this age-old method where the sculler stood in the boat a hangover from the Elizabethan ferryman?

The varnished mainmast was stepped in an iron box called a luchet or a tabernacle which was painted green, the symbolic colour of birth, life and energy. From the cross trees main runners stretched to the rails, up which generations of apprentices had been sent with knocking knees and vertigo to survey a very small deck and an awful lot of water. Flying at the very top was the 'bob' to indicate wind direction, not decorate the topmast, although some bore the colours of their owners; in Dickens' day it might have been the white horse of a Kentish cement company; in recent days it was more likely to be the yellow of Portland Cement.

It was from the mast that all life surged, and whilst the amount of canvas a barge carried depended on what she was doing, the basics alone could add up to 3,000 square feet. The distinctive red colour was achieved once again, for purely practical purposes. The sails, originally of Egyptian cotton, were spread out on the grass of a sunny day, and a mixture of horse-grease, tar and yellow ochre was heated, mixed with sea-water and rubbed well in, then a coating of linseed oil was added, which gave them a wettish feel. The sails were never allowed to dry right out which made handling them much easier in a stiff breeze, and of course, helped them to last that much longer. When many barges were stripped during the war and their sails safely stowed – or so it was thought – they were found to be useless when brought out again, because they had dried out in four years of inactivity and the canvas had rotted.

Working the windlass.

The amount and design of sail, the boat's length and tonnage, created many variations, but three things remained constant on all those barges of the Thames: their sail colour, the lee-boards, and the 'sprit' or 'spreet' which originated again with the Dutch. There was no spar or swinging boom on the mainsail to crack a man's skull; instead the sprit or pole ran diagonnaly upwards from one foot to the mast where it was housed in a great iron collar, and its topmost end 'at 10 minutes to twelve', was attached to the topmast by a headrope, which from a distance made the mainsail look as if it was suspended in thin air. Before 1800 the average barge would have carried only a foresail and mainsail, but then along came the sprit to increase performance – though it often got carried away. As the length of hull grew and more sail was needed, a whole gamut of new ideas appeared: gaff sail, jib-headed top sails and so on, so that the coastal barge also made a first class racing vessel.

The earlier rigging was usually tarred hemp, but after the industrial revolution, it was largely replaced by wire. Another Dutch feature was the vang, pronounced 'wang', two wire braces to control the angle of the sail which stretched down from the 'peak' of the sprit to the rails. Finally there were the brails, which reminded me so much of theatre curtains. The mainsail was connected to the mast by three rings of wire and rope which enabled one man to shorten sail without all the jumble of lowering or 'reefing' it, that moment when the average sailing boat looks like a pile of flapping laundry and the yachtsman wishes he had eight arms. Practical as ever, the brails also helped in the stowing of a sail, for when it was lowered it tended to layer in a neat concertina.

Almost everything then, was there to make the vessel manageable with the minimum of crew, in most cases just the skipper and his mate, and the mate was very often a fourteen-year-old boy, or the skipper's wife. Occasionally the larger vessels venturing over the Channel would take on an extra hand. But I couldn't help wondering at a weekend enthusiasts' barge excursion with her crew of eight, just whether the muscle power and endurance would be there today.

However, thus far I had looked only at the exterior of the barge, the business end. It was the personal I was after, and a nose between decks at the interior which had shaped so much of a sailorman's life was a must.

The snuggest part of the vessel was its main cabin, called a 'cuddy'. It was usually about ten or twelve feet long, with bunks on either side, starboard side for the skipper. The bunks were built into fine panelling, often of highly polished maple or mahogany, and were usually slid shut during the daytime, so that the effect was rather like sleeping in a cupboard, or as it was morbidly known, a coffin, often affording the only privacy a man had. At the stern was a long built-in seat, universally known as the 'Yarmouth Roads', probably because if the barge was shipping any water the damp would congregate there. In front of that would be a communal table, often again of fine timber and around it a couple of benches with the wood for the fire stacked beneath them. Overhead a small skylight and rather fine brass oil-lamps swung on gymbals. At the forward end of the cabin stood a small stove, very often richly cast in ornate iron-work, with double doors which could be opened out, and occasionally a range on which could be boiled the delicious traditional stews and duffs.

An apprentice soon learned not to stoke the fire till it spat or roared as, apart from the danger of a blaze, it was believed to invoke a storm. And that wasn't all the boys had to learn about the cuddy. Watermen's superstitions ran deep, but with a strong basis of plain common sense, as sailing barge man Charlie Jackson recalls:

> Never leave anything on a vessel upside down. You wouldn't half get a belt from the Old Man if he saw yer fo'c'sle hatch upside down. Ladders, and tin cans – food, that sort of thing – they were never stowed upside down – baked beans and that. Boat hooks and belaying pins were always stowed tucked underneath and facing forrard, and nobody was happy bunking down with sharp knives open to the sky – they were always wrapped in cloth or put away. 'Cause, it was common sense – you could lose your hatch cover, trip over a sharp boat hook, get a crick in yer neck reading a tin up the wrong way, get a bruise on your bum or cut yer finger off in the dark, but it went deeper than that – it wasn't just practical – it was bad luck, and you didn't tempt providence.

Dick Virgo agreed:

> We was as worldly as most, but for all that, if anything did go wrong, the first thing one of us would do would be to leg it really sharp below to see if tins or anything else was upside down, and be sure I breathed a bit lighter if it was all shipshape down there.

If the barge was a big one, the skipper might have his own state room aft, but it was usually extremely small with hardly enough room to undress in. There was rarely a wheelhouse; perhaps forward, a cabin in the forecastle for the extra hands on sea runs; this was really more of a store-room or rope-locker where hanging cots could be slung.

So the barges fell into two main classes, the coastal and the river barge. Naturally the coastal would be bigger, on average between 120 to 180 tons, and carry much more sail for speed – hence the bowsprit and topmast. The river trader's speed was not so important as her capacity. However, within these two classes there were a dozen or so variations, and a sailorman in a long career would, of course, have served on all of them at one time or another.

All those barges which were likely to ply above bridge were known generally as stumpies; they were narrower in 1903 and shorter and had no topmast or topsail. The stumpie was the real old packhorse, the beast of burden which Erskine Pollock in 1903 claimed had created the Port of London. She carried mostly coal or coke (which is why Battersea, Southwark and all the other power stations are close to the river), and the smellier freights of garbage to the screaming accompaniment of great flocks of gulls and millions of flies. Several skippers I was to talk to had sad memories of this job, when with work short, the statelier coastal barges had resorted to this too. It's a sobering thought that these beautiful vessels were reduced to transporting 22,000 concrete piles and untold tons of rubbish for the land reclamation on which Fords Motor Works at Dagenham were built in 1929 to produce the very machines which were to cause their eclipse. From Wellington Wharf and elsewhere came fleets of 'brickies', and the Kentish brickfields alone employed fleets of 100 ton vessels each stowing an average of 42,000 bricks, some of them from Haling which discarded the traditional red mainsail for a black one bearing the rampant horse of Kent. Millions of tons of bricks poured out of the Kentish and Essex brickfields for the great expansion of London with their embossed 'J.W.s' for John Woods and the 'B.B.B.B.' for Butcher's Bricks. To navigate somewhere like the Regents Canal the complaining mates of an Eastwood's barge, more used to open waters, had to lie on their backs to 'leg it' through the tunnels between Regents Park and Marylebone.

The stumpie found herself in all sorts of places, carrying every kind of cargo. It was not unusual to come up river with a load of cement and then have to clean the holds from top to bottom for grain, a profitless labour, because a crew was only paid for the cargo

Unloading cement from the Will Everard. *If the next cargo was grain, there was a big cleaning out job afterwards.*

carrying. A typical sight on the Thames would have been the stackie with its wider beam, shallower sides and draught and a curiously pointed stern called a nipcat which had nosed its way to the harvest fields of Kent and Essex to load with huge bales of hay for the thousands of horses that once powered tram-cars and conveyances of every kind. These were often piled so high that the skipper's view was completely blocked by a mountain of hay and the mate would always be seen sitting on top and 'conning' for him. The stumpie was a marvellously economic business, for it would ply up to London with hay, and return to the farmers loaded with manure for their fields, and many of these transactions were effected by barter rather than cash.

In the deserted creeks and inlets might be seen a sandie, small barges which specialised in collecting silver sand which was used uptown for sanding floors and scouring tables and bars. The sandie men were a taciturn lot and not averse to a little sheep stealing off the marshes. The London barge kid, down with his Dad at Egypt Bay or St. Mary's Bay who watched them 'gitting' with their back-breaking wooden shovel, called a fly tool, was in for a hefty clump round the ear, if he was cheeky enough to shout "Baaa!" to a sandie.

In earlier days the chalkies from the Kentish Downs brought tons of chalk to the fields of Essex to lighten its heavy soil. Many of these barge skippers were not considered master mariners, and in fact carried no papers at all, so that upriver, away from their element in crowded waters, they were commonly put down by licensed watermen and river pilots. However, in 1835, one illiterate chalkie skipper and his mate, who were in collison with a 500 ton vessel, the *Baron Holberg*, off Woolwich Reach were cleared by an investigating enquiry, so they must have known what they were doing both above and below bridge. Some barges, smaller in general than others, were entirely crewed by Irishmen and were known as paddy boats, and another popular sight must have been the brewery barges, their skippers – many of them staunch teetotallers – heaving a sigh of relief as they rounded the bend and saw Southwark Brewery Wharf, for they had to sleep with one eye open en route, and nobody has really explained the mystery of the *Miller* which collided with the *Genesta* when her entire freight of beer simply disappeared into thin air.

The entire length of the Thames was at one time dotted with gunpowder works, and earning every penny were the skippers of the gunpowder barges with their bright red paintwork, as if anybody needed a hint to give them a wide berth.

These then, were a few of the types on which both western and London bargemen would work in the great days of the barge, before the timber would be cheaper to obtain abroad, and the steel barge, inboard engine and Dutch motor vessel had planted the seeds of decline. A look at some of the names given to the barges, reads like Britain's own history. The boat-builder with paint brush poised in 1901, reads of a little Italian's invention which sends a message from Signal Hill to Newfoundland via a primitive kite aerial, and a barge runs down the slips as *Marconi*. Another picks up his newspaper on May 17th, 1900 and *Mafeking* weighs anchor, perhaps passing *Lord Roberts* as she drudges downstream. Grandiose names such as *Wellington*, *Baden-Powell*, *Lord Haig* rub shoulders with barges named after wives, or sweethearts, such as *Veronica*, *Priscilla*, *Sara* and *Lucy*. Those of the Everards' fleet were all named after members of the family. Indeed, so attached to their barges were some skippers, that the process was reversed, and one man even christened his daughter Francis [sic] of London.

Thames Traffic

Standing one summer's day on the Tower slip
Careless how I my time should employ,
It popp'd in my head that I'd take a trip
Aboard a Margate hoy.

THE BARGEMAN PLYING his trade up and down the Thames would encounter a great many other working boats each day. He might pass sailing boats, wherries, hoys, colliers or a wide variety of fishing vessels. A hay bargeman coming from his peace or 'samp' in a Kent inlet would in a few short hours be transported into all the clanking cacophony or 'chirm' of the Pool of London. He must have experienced disturbing symptoms not unlike those of a sleeper suddenly thrown into a waking nightmare when iron monsters gushing steam and oil threatened to chew up his barge.

The little scudding hoys of Charles Dibden's 1770s were still around but in most cases, by the middle of the nineteenth century, they had been replaced by paddle steamers. The hoys with their rigging like a sloop might disappear but their memory will always remain with us for do we not still shout 'Ahoy!' when we wish to hail a boat for a lift?

The paddle steamers were splendid affairs, all gleaming brasswork, hissing pistons, iron paddles and white scrubbed decks. All were owned by independent companies and competition was so great that it was a wonder more collisions did not take place as each rushed for the crowded quaysides in order to pick up fares waiting at Customs House and London Bridge Wharf. Those which went above London Bridge had curiously lop-sided funnels which could be lowered to shoot the arches, others went down river to the Channel ports, whilst their passengers turned slowly green as the swell rose.

By an Act of Parliament of 1763, a master could be fined for not keeping to the timetable, and on top of the churning colliers, hay barges, merchantmen and fishing boats surging to make Billingsgate and its fish and coal quays, paddle steamers of the Citizen Steamboat Company, the Iron Boat Co., and the Westminster Steamboat Company wrestled for place alongside those of the Southend and Margate Packets who twisted back and forth through the narrow bottle-neck crowded with passengers.

Dickens' Jack-of-the water, on replying to his enquiry whether the packet *Endeavour* had 'gone up yet?' replied, "I should think she's gawn down by this time, for she's a precious sight too full of ladies and gen'lemen!" Weaving in and out of all this lot like a demented mosquito was the General Steamboat Navigation Company's diamond packet which called at London Bridge Wharf, the Tunnel by nine o'clock, then Greenwich, Woolwich, Erith and Southend Piers, as announced with great jubilation by *The Times* on May 8th, 1847. At Woolwich the Penny Ferry was punching smelly punctuation marks back and forth across the river to the consternation of free-flying schooners and cutters trying to take advantage of a favourable wind. When the customary bells rang at London Bridge to signal high tide, the scene must have looked like the start of some insane race, the big paddles churning up all the muck and sewerage over which the barge glided undisturbed, so that ladies swooned and handkerchiefs were wrapped round puce faces:

"Go on!" cried the Master of the boat from the top of one of the paddle-boxes.

"Go on!" echoed the boy, who was stationed over the hatchway to pass instructions down to the engineer; and away went the vessel with that agreeable noise which is peculiar to steamers and which is composed of a pleasant mixture of creaking, gushing, clanging and snorting . . . the boat starts; people who have been taking their leave of their friends on board, are carried away against their will; and people who have been taking leave of their friends on shore, find that they have performed a very needless ceremony in consequence of their not being carried away at all. The regular passengers who have season tickets go below to breakfast; people who have purchased morning papers compose themselves to read them; and people who have not been downriver before, think that both the shipping and the water, look a great deal better at a distance.

(Charles Dickens, *Sketches by 'Boz'*)

Steam excursion according to Cruikshank in Sketches by 'Boz'.

1875 marked the inauguration of yet another company, the London Steamboat to Gravesend and Sheerness, and also, incidentally, a five mile swim by a fourteen-year-old riverside girl, Ann Beckworth, who that September did the trip from London Bridge to Greenwich in one hour eight minutes and doesn't seem to have had many contenders for her title.

Something was bound to happen with so many paddle steamers jostling one another and not three years later, on Tuesday September 3rd, 1878, fate emphasised the sheer lunacy of so many vessels packing unsupervised into such a narrow reach as Gallion's. The *Princess Alice* was an iron saloon steamer returning from Sheerness with some 900 people aboard her, and she left to posterity the three great symbols of the industrial revolution: steam, coal and muck, which combined to make one of the biggest disasters the people of Charlton had ever witnessed.

One of the most succinct witnesses of the catastrophe, was a sailorman who had been ousted by steam, and was a passenger aboard the *Princess Alice* when she collided. Finding himself with a day spare, G. W. Linnecar, a sailorman turned preacher, had caught the steamer down to Rosherville Gardens, a favourite spot for outings at Gravesend. He had struck up a friendship with a young couple who had married that day and were enjoying a twenty-four-hour honeymoon before returning to work. The *Princess Alice* was only 220 feet long and twenty feet wide, and when she sailed she was so crowded that "there was no such thing as walking about – you had to be content with either sitting or standing and forming a little part of the solid mass". The journey passed uneventfully until they reached that old hazard, Gallion's Reach, when Linnecar, with a professional eye seemed to have a premonition as they rounded 'the devil's elbow'.

As a man who had spent years at sea, I naturally kept a sharp eye on these dangerous parts of the river, and I was looking along the stretch of water known as Gallion's, when I saw a screw steamboat coming towards us. She was for those days a fairly big vessel, being about 1,400 tons . . . she seemed to stand very high in the water, for she was in ballast, and was what sailormen call 'flying light' . . . I was playing with some children . . . With laughter still in my heart I looked ahead and saw the *Bywell Castle* actually looming over our starboard bow. She looked like a great monster which was deliberately coming up to strike her prey . . . the captain had just passed me . . . I sprang up onto a form and shouted "She'll be into us!" Almost before the words were out of my mouth the great bow had crashed into the side of us, just by the starboard sponson, which is the wooden platform jutting out from the paddle-box. The *Bywell Castle* drove into the very heart of the *Princess Alice* just as a strong knife might be driven through a matchbox . . . the collier cut through as far as the engine room, and literally doubled us up and smashed us into two pieces . . . all of us seemed to drop down like skittles. Then there was a terrific struggle both on deck and in the water.

Riverside families at Woolwich rushed into all the boats that they could lay hands on in order to save as many people as possible. Linnecar continues:

Everything that was within reach was seized and held in convulsive grips . . . women and children rolled over and clutched and tore at each other . . . I saw the only hope for me lay in reaching the deck of the *Bywell Castle*. The collier herself was little damaged because, as a rule, it is the vessel which is run into which suffers, especially when, as in our case, she is struck amidships . . . I glanced swiftly about me and saw that there was only one way of reaching the collier's deck, and that was to swarm up one of the chains supporting the funnels of the *Princess Alice* and clamber from the top of it to the *Bywell Castle* – the bow of which was still sticking into the dreadful gaping wound . . . How I did it to this day I do not know, but in my frenzy and despair I swarmed up the funnel-guy just as in my earlier days at sea I had climbed aloft . . . Look at this thumb of mine – see the scar upon it? How the wound came there I cannot tell you . . . my sea-training helped me to do what I could not have done if I had been a landsman.'

By this time many of the riverside wherries and other rescue craft had reached the wallowing vessel, but panic had set in, and many of the women in their voluminous skirts were dragged under, some just disappeared from sight; others mad with panic actually fought away the helping hands attempting to pull them inboard. Linnecar himself tried to lower the collier's lifeboats, which were rusted and set, but most of the efforts and advice shouted from watermen were unheeded. Suddenly with what witnesses called 'a death rattle', the anchor chain of the ship began to slide into the water, carrying with it screaming people who had been attempting to climb up, or who were clinging round the hawse-hole. The anchor was dropped, and people simply disappeared in living chains of oil-soaked bodies.

The wreck of the Princess Alice, *1879, below and opposite.*

Whoever gave the order, or whether the slipping of the anchor chain was a pure accident, will never be known, but *Princess Alice* slowly disappeared, and the local people rowed some 700 corpses ashore to be laid out at Woolwich Pier where next of kin collected to identify their own in a melancholy scene which lasted for days. Linnecar himself, soaking wet and badly gashed, hailed a cabbie. But the cabbie wanted a guinea to take him home, so Linnecar dragged himself off by train, still holding the return ticket which he kept to the day he died, although the printing was completely obliterated by water-stains.

The incident stirred the public, and perhaps for the first time, the 'townie' upriver was made aware that there was another community 'round the bend', and that many of the people who died might have lived if the river had not been so filthy from the southern outfall sewer – a point which locals had been trying to make for years. With the captain of the *Princess Alice* blamed for negligence, it was obvious

that the London Steamship Company's days were numbered, and the company went into liquidation in 1884. However, with a hard lesson learned, the other paddle steamers carried on.

By 1824 fishing as a staple downriver had waned, for in that year Francis Place reported that, "Fishing in the River . . . is not as good a trade as it was . . . ten years ago." However, if fishing on a large scale had retreated, there was no dearth of small local fishing vessels on the Thames, each one specialising in its own particular method. The Hewlett family operated a fishing fleet out of Barking and also did a roaring trade in the preservation of ice for Billingsgate. Where Abbey Road runs now, there ran an ingenious system of traps (learnt from the Romans) by which the ice was caught in winter, then preserved in huge ice houses. In the 1850s the Hewletts had a fleet of 180 vessels, and the area claimed to be the cradle of the trawling industry. But in the terrible storms of 1863, sixty local fishermen died, and the little community never really recovered. Bethnal Green had its own fishing fleet, and for years attempted to keep going under the ownership of Baroness Burdett-Coutts. Off Greenwich and Woolwich, too, stood small fleets which were gradually dispersing

Greenwich beach in the 1900s.

reenwich Beach.

to the lucrative fishing fields of the east coast and further, for local rumour has it that Greenwich men formed the nucleus of the deep-sea Hull trawler fleets.

The power of omens among the Thames fishing fleets was strong, and often with a different significance to the landsman's interpretation. A black cat crossing a path ashore was good luck, aboard a vessel it heralded a storm. The sight of a hare near the quayside could stop a fishing fleet from sailing, and a hare's foot thrown on to a fishing vessel would arouse the kind of hysteria one associates with ju-ju dolls in Africa. For some inexplicable reason, fishermen also hated white stones in their ballast, and this had to be carefully sifted before loading, just as holed stones were discarded, as they meant a holed net. If a monk fish was caught, it was always nailed to the mast as a warning to evil forces to stay away – in effect the mariner's parallel to the countrymen of Kent, who still kill carrion crows and hang them on fences to warn off others.

For years people believed in the Royal King Herring which was said to have evolved from the sea-anemone, and which served man by driving the shoals into his net. The King Herring is still honoured by riverside folk who will still carefully rearrange the backbone and skeleton of a herring after eating it, and wrap it in paper before throwing it back into the water in the belief that King Herring, with a little help from his friends, will reconstitute the carcass into a plump new fish. They also eat the fish from tail to head in obedience to an inherited old maxim that a fish eaten from head to tail will cause future shoals to turn tail and head back out to sea away from the nets.

In the 1850s the riverborne traveller would have seen an interesting array of little fishing vessels working off Woolwich Reach, and adding, no doubt, to the perilous congestion there. Harry Thomas Harris for one had a slim opinion of their skill, and a clumsy lighterman had been given a stinging 'put down' indeed if he ever got himself dubbed 'as awkward as a fisherman'. Many of these local men were members of the Company of Free Fishermen of the River Thames which had been formed in 1697, and there was a good deal of rivalry between them and the Essex men, for the river rights ran as far as Stansgate.

A view of Greenwich engraved around 1840 shows local fishermen at Greenwich marsh in their canvas 'skirts' and long hair stuffed into droopy caps – an overall appearance not unlike garden-gnomes.

In the shallows lie three London peter boats. A unique little craft, peculiar to London waters, and a descendent of the medieval cromster, they were twenty to thirty feet long, and gave the curious appearance of going neither forward nor backward, having two 'sharp' ends. They were a common sight from London Bridge to Yantlet Creek, often sporting finely carved transoms, smoke curling up from a single little chimney poking through dark blankets which were stretched over a small arched shelter forrard and called a 'tilton tail'. Some of these frail little craft would go out for a week or longer single-handed. The peter net, a small-skein net about twenty fathoms long, was hurled out after two twirls over the head to surround a shoal of fish in midstream. The catch was kept fresh for market either in a small well inboard, or towed astern in a fish box known as a 'koff'.

The peter boat man's main catch was whitebait, a popular and staple dish, and the Ship and Trafalgar at Greenwich did a roaring trade cooking them. He also caught shrimps in nets called 'trinkers' during the season which ran from the opening to closing of Parliament. It was in the shrimping area that the peter boat man ran headlong into war with the Leigh fisherman further downriver, for it invaded their monopoly. Eventually the Leigh fisherman developed the peter boat's design into a larger vessel known as a 'bawley' from the boiler in which he boiled his catch on its way to market. The war still raged as late as 1893 so Thames Conservancy bye-laws forbade these Leigh bawleys fishing above Sea-Reach at Southend which promptly ousted Greenwich as the centre for both shrimp and whitebait. The very long pier there was originally built to enable a quick turn round for market. The peter net fisherman from London was also engaged in spratting, these 'minims of the sea' forming one of the few sources of protein to London's poor. They were also exported in huge quantities to Germany, Holland, Russia and Norway (now we buy theirs).

However, where the peter boat fisherman really parted company with the conservationists was in his activities along the shoreline, and though he himself has disappeared, he has bequeathed many of these illegal practices to the sailorman in his barge. Kettling was a technique by which a net with a pocket was stretched over the estuary of a small creek, and the fish, irrespective of size, driven down into it. The netting enclosures were called kettles, kiddles or trim-trams, and were stretched over high and low water mark. If a man could get away without being caught, he developed a more elaborate system of stakes with lines of little rings which would jangle noisily to herd his catch into the kettle, and the practice has not entirely died out, for the estuary on the Kent side still reveals the occasional little row of stakes forming a small weir with the pit of a sunken keep-box for storage of live fish close by. A valuable catch, such as a turbot, often had a cork tied round its tail for easy reference. All this was made illegal in the 1860s but whole successions of bargemen chose to ignore the ruling. We spent many holidays on the marshland creeks trapping shrimps and prawns by this method, and we were never alone.

Once a year at its annual fair, Greenwich became the 'emporium of shrimps and reservoir of beer' to thousands of Cockneys who flocked to their annual beanfeast there, and serving this huge demand for millions of shrimps were the bawleys from Leigh-on-Sea, their fishermen dressed in plum-coloured trews and white ducks on the Sabbath. The vessel had a straight stem rather like a rowing boat, and no boom so that it could be handled beautifully by two men. Bawley men and sailormen had a strong respect for each other, and annual races of bawleys took place right up to the 1920s. Their history, however, had a shadier side, for until the arrival of fast Naval cutters and organised surveillance, the Leigh men were not averse to a little dark work. If fishing was bad, and gathering 'duckson' (a weed for manure) began to pall, there was always a little smuggling or running in contraband from a larger vessel. The 'moonraker' legends originated around the Leigh-on-Sea coastline. Contraband was submerged by day, and retrieved by night so that the men appeared to be 'raking the moon's reflection' as they retrieved their goods. There was also a saying in Leigh that if you wanted some coal you just 'pray'd for a nor'-easter', and whilst wrecking was on nothing like the scale of the West Country, there are reports of Leigh men showing false lights behind sandbanks.

Another vessel that might be seen scudding past the barge sailormen, was the dandy-rigged cod smack from Harwich, its sailors leaning over the rails in their tight bell-bottoms of velveteen, pilot jackets and jerseys with uniform black silk handkerchiefs, hand-made knee boots and cheese-cutters. Their cod nets were treated with oak bark and dog-fish oil which gave their vessels and clothes a strange tang. By 1863 there were only ninety-seven left, the railways having bitten deep into their London trade. Perhaps there was a Brighton 'hoggy' with a lee-board like a barge, or a Plymouth 'long boomer', Falmouth 'quay punt', or a Mounts Bay 'drifter' – all with a quite distinct show of sail.

All men of sail were united, however, in cursing the new grunting steam colliers or 'flat-irons' which necessitated constant avoiding tacking, for still in 1844, three-quarters of the colliers were sail, and employed over 10,000 seamen – some 8,000 manoeuvring the Thames with 2½ million tons of coal. Records at Custom House recorded 8,600 tons brought in in one single day of 1854. There would also be several little 'cats' or coal carrying boats from Ipswich, and in the summer when trade slackened, dozens of them could be seen hauled up on the shore, their rigging stripped and crews presumably left to their own devices.

There were oyster smacks from the East Anglian beds where the age-old technique was adapted from the Romans, who taught Brightlingsea people the secrets of oyster fattening, and in 1850 with 144 million sold on the streets of London alone at four for a penny, the demand was still enormous. However it wasn't only an east coast trade. Lots of people in Kent collected oysters and cockles in their own boats, many of which were old warship galleys, purchased from the Naval Breakers' yard nearby at Sheerness, and they could be seen up many a creek and gulley, their small makeshift cuddies giving them a top-heavy appearance. Indeed, it is only recently, with the disappearance of the railway to Allhallows, that the enterprising coster has stopped his weekly excursions down to the cockle and winkle gatherer to buy them and return to the Smoke in time for the Londoner's afternoon tea and a thriving street trade on Sundays.

The best oysters came from the wide open mud-flats of the Blackwater estuary near Mersea in Essex and now one lone survivor continues the tradition, the Mussent family. Toughest of the oyster-men, were the 'skillers' who brought in oysters off the dangerous grounds of the Frisian Islands, and amongst whom constant feuds over disputed grounds raged and called for Naval intervention on more than one occasion.

Most of the estuary man's murkier history has died with his vessel, the Kentish or Essex smack which was such a common sight. Ostensibly classed as fishers, these smacks also formed the earliest lifeboats that a mariner in difficulty could look to for help; often indeed the help was unsolicited. Where above-bridge pilfering was on the scale of a few quid a time, down here the thieves would carry off the entire boat given half a chance. Reports abounded of lone vessels being surrounded rather ominously by smacks 'in case' the skipper needed help. Captain Garrick of the London brig *Lochiel* had his vessel stripped to the bones at Sheerness. In 1852 a Scottish schooner, *Renown*, got into difficulties on the Nore, and dozens of little Southend smacks, not surprisingly known as 'vultures', swarmed out to 'render assistance'. A Sheerness gunboat had to save the captain when he was down to his underpants. In 1879 a Norwegian barque *Nef* was boarded by solicitous life-savers who took off the crew and everything else they could lay hands on, including the brass handles and door-hinges. However the 'vultures' did save life too, and in the 1870s when a German emigrant ship foundered on Grain Spit, a local man, Tom Barnard, in his *New Unity* ferried off all the passengers safely, receiving an award for his efforts – ironically, however, he lost his smack some years later on the same spit.

Smuggling was a way of life developed as a reaction in the days when taxes and customs were imposed on people who saw no reason for them, and it has never died out. Ships were built with hollow masts and barges held secret compartments in their cuddies, though few builders can have so muddled their priorities as Sainty's of Wivenhoe, who built a fast smuggling vessel, *Wolverine*, which became the scourge of the east coast, until she was forced by an equally speedy Naval cutter into a cave at Beachy Head and blown up. It was another Sainty brother who had built the Naval vessel which overtook her. One enterprising bargeman, John Bridges, sailed gaily past revenue cutters with his linen sacks of peas – until they realised that it was the linen he was running.

"There are upwards of 30 sail cutters constantly employed in smuggling between Naze Point and the Mouth of the Thames . . . which carry on with impunity a great trade in the rivers and creeks," reported the Collector of Customs in 1777, and when we realise that something as innocuous as soap was dutiable until 1835, this clandestine activity is not surprising. On the Allhallows side casks were brought ashore and hidden in Kentish dene holes. These were often old chalk mines, always bottle-shaped, with a small entrance widening to larger chambers and tunnels. There were dozens of them over Kent and Essex. In the 1820s workmen digging the Gravesend to Stroud canal found a tunnel running from under a waterside mill at Denton to Gravesend. There is supposed to be

Muddies loading a barge on the Medway. The skipper and his mate look on.

another under the roadway in Allhallows village which runs from the pub to the churchyard. Yantlet Creek is also a favourite landing spot; goods could be landed on Gantlebor Island, a mud flat lying off the creek. The little bays and inlets around the Lower Hope were also used for illegal boxing matches for the gentry with very high stakes. Still today, along dozens of little creeks lone pubs stand close to the water, and it wasn't because the western bargeman hated to 'snudge' (walk) any great distance for his 'niggle' ('waxer' to the upriver man). It was because, as another report went, "Each public house on the . . . mainland near a creek, obtained its entire supply of wine and spirits from contraband vessels. Whether the coastguards were bought to shut their eyes or were baffled by the adroitness of the smugglers, cannot be said, but the taverns found no difficulty in obtaining supplies as often and as abundantly as they desired."

Laws came in in 1816 by which vessels such as cutters, luggers, wherries, sloops, smacks and yawls were not allowed to have bowsprits of more than two-thirds their own length, and a boat of more than four oars – except for licensed watermen – was liable to seizure. No lights were to be shown as signals from ship to shore, and for some peculiar reason, the sailorman's 'warmer' of chocolate or cocoa was forbidden on board ship. Soldiers manned martello towers, and old hulks were used as watch vessels, but despite such vigilance illicit trade continued on a grand scale. In 1849 *Charlotte* was caught off Gravesend with no less than 14,402 pounds of undeclared tobacco. Fishermen commonly hid their contraband baccy in a barrel of rotten fish to dissuade nosy rummagers, and bargemen developed a fine line in sea-boots with concealed piping inside them. Penalties were heavy, however, and Dickens wrote of the marshes, "On the edge of the river I could faintly make out the only two black things in all the prospect that seemed to be standing upright. One of these was a beacon by which the sailors steered . . . the other a gibbet with some chains hanging on it."

❦ 10 ❦

In Living Memory

The race is not always got
By them that strive and for it run,
Nor the battle to them people
Wot's got the longest gun.

ALL THE DELVING thus far, except for the occasional light thrown by
written reminiscences of a riverside personality, is but the anatomy,
the skeletal remains of the past, the events which fashioned inherited
family outlook and prejudice. It came as something of a shock to me
to discover how quickly the riverside we see today has taken shape,
and hitherto, I had not really grasped completely what a shuddering
impact the industrial revolution had had on what, less than 130 years
ago, had been a string of proud little communities, nor how the
enormous tide of newcomers had so infiltrated and fundamentally
changed the character and identity of those communities.

However some attitudes had been explained – the basic suspicion
and barely disguised antipathy towards all riverside landowners;
insistence still that south of the river is bound only to London by the
Greater London Council, but by no traditional links; the instinctive,
though overt admiration for the smuggler, the fellow who bends the
rules, the character who dares to challenge the Establishment.

Grandad was born in a back room at 31, Henrietta Street, Bethnal
Green on May 1st 1883, his birth certificate shakily signed by my
great-grandfather, Edward, and Sara Ann Waskell who made her
simple cross. The attitudes to life I had been discovering explained
why he turned his back on the grunting steam-yards where his father

toiled as a wheelwright's smith, in favour of the relative freedom of the water, as an apprentice at Battersea Barge Roads, and why his brother Jack jumped ship in Australia in search of a better life.

With motives explained, and background etched into place, it seemed time to home in on the area where immediate family reminiscences started, for the trail was leading me to Charlton Riverside where Grandfather had moved after marrying a Sullivan from the Irish quarter upriver. However, when I went to all the usual places where you would expect to find information, the cupboard was bare, except for a few dry maps like General Booth's. He had etched the area in a colour which signified 'moderately poor inhabitants' for the Salvation Army. In dozens of guide books, copious paragraphs glowed with the glamorous past of Greenwich Palace, Blackheath and Woolwich, but nothing of Riverside – it was like looking at a doughnut with a hole in the middle.

Perhaps, like Pepys, successive chroniclers had been scared of going down there; the place was rough enough right to the time the bulldozers moved in. Even the doughty Mayhew seemed to have had enough to occupy him in Rotherhithe and the Whitechapel Road, and Gustave Doré had filled his sketchbooks with too many river-siders at Greenwich Palace to warrant the muddy trudge down the Woolwich Road. However, people there had been, since the Saxons came, friends, neighbours, enemies, for high days and holidays, and since the anatomy and the history were dovetailing into the beginning of the twentieth century and therefore within living memory, it seemed time to meet at first hand the people who had lived through those times and could provide the flesh and blood, the sights and sounds where Grandad had hung his hat.

'The river was our oyster and we learnt to swim amongst the skipjacks.'
1914.

On an overcast day heavy with the threat of rain in October 1977, I took the train down to Charlton to walk what was left of the once crowded Riverside – that small rectangle bounded by the four streets – Anchor and Hope Lane, Riverside, Hardens Manor Way and the Woolwich Road, their outermost boundary marked by the Waterman's Arms.

The four streets around 1900: Cox's Mount in foreground, with Maryon Park School, right; Hardens Manor Way leads down the meadow towards the river; left centre, the Lads of the Village pub and the East Street Mission; Siemen's, centre, and the top masts of Warspite *behind the works.*

To visualise ranks of two-up two-downers with their little corner shops sweet with the smell of barrelled beans and new baked bread, home-made toffee and fresh herring was something I had to do with half-closed eyes, for they were gone, reduced to dry open wastelands of demolition site visible through rusting corrugated iron. The community in which my family had grown up was now scattered over the metropolis – many of them rehoused above Charlton Heights. The four bordering pubs still stood, and the Woolwich Road, which had been the dividing line between the riverside people and more genteel houses of the city clerks and other white collar workers, was busy with passing traffic intent on getting somewhere else.

From there ran Anchor and Hope Lane clear to the river, at its end, the Anchor & Hope pub, now run by a chain brewery, a manager instead of a waterman landlord, and no hint of the past about its forlorn walls. The racks on which prized racing skiffs had been housed were gone, and the projecting balcony where proud parents had watched their sons resplendent in red coats for the Doggett's Coat and Badge, had disappeared. Following the towpath of Riverside on my right I passed crumbling jetties, rusting lighters, and two wherries rotting in the mud. The forbidding frontage of Siemen's Works loomed, partially demolished, the air heavy with the smell of decay and damp, the ground treacherous with fallen masonry and puddles of glutinous wet plaster. Between the disused sites stood small workshops, and a modern prefabricated factory plant where all the little houses of West Street had jostled for air, their small rose gardens and cabbage patches submerged under discarded bricks. Every so often an articulated lorry manoeuvred into high-walled yards, its sides scouring the narrow passages which had been built to admit a man with a barrow or drays drawing cullet wagons.

In the whole walk along Riverside, I met not a soul. The only sign of life came from a new pier and the office of Sargent Brothers at the foot of Hardens Manor Way, and through an open window came the sound of an intercom radio calling up Gallion's. Back inland along Hardens Manor Way, the ugly towers of the Thames Barrage were rusting in the work site. This street had formed the boundary of Greenwich and Woolwich, and to my right had stood number 44 where Grandad had lived for a spell. Then he had looked out at a wide meadow where the kids had played football amongst the rhubarb patches. At the top stood the sad little school where the local populace had mugged up their three Rs, and The Lads of the Village pub, bright with new paint, one or two tables outside, but no sign of the terrace of houses of which it had formed but one small part. A door opened and an old man came out, dog at his side. He stopped to lock the door securely and then looked round at the ugly corrugated iron from which an old tree, scarred with countless initials, struggled to the sky. Then he was gone into East Street.

I walked on to West Street where the family had moved, trying hard to picture the way the back gardens had met each other over little fences and bright hedges. Where the nursery fields had once stood behind West Street, more barbed wire, and the only standing wharfinger's building in North Street gave some indication of the congestion these four streets had once known, the cobbles once loud with the echoing clatter of horses' hooves, and shipwrights' mallets. Back towards Anchor and Hope Lane, a small knot of isolated houses were still inhabited, but for the rest it was going to be no easy job to infuse even the tiniest hint of past life. Beyond, the task remained no easier – the huge garrison at Woolwich where the noonday guns had fired, and streets had been bright with soldiers in their best walking-out finery, the eel-pie shops, drysalters, chandlers, telescope-makers, victuallers, and noisy seamen's digs had gone.

Kelly's Directory for 1920 put some names to the plots inhabited now by nettles and rubbish. In West Street had lived the Walkers, Dytes, Bucklands, Mrs. Richards the Sweet at number 17; the Etheringtons, Gruskers, Chapmans, Rileys, Sullivans (so the barriers of the Irish quarter had come down), Smalls, Samuels the boot repairers, Lodders, Luxfords, Wallaces, Thatchers, Garlicks, Swales, Olivers . . . 181 little boxes with unrecorded broods of children, and paper-thin walls where everybody knew everybody else's business. In North Street, more names, their back windows overlooking the river, and one was Jackson.

Retired now after a lifetime as a Thames Sailing Barge sailorman, Charlie Jackson admitted me to his small front parlour in Prince Henry Road, two streets from where we had congregated at Grandad's house for our Sunday teas twenty years ago. He recalled the area in the early decades of the century. The living memories had started.

Off Woolwich Church Street was what we called 'Forty Corners'; Gas House Alley, Shorts Alley, The Grove, Hog Lane (they did keep pigs there one time), Sow Alley, Pig Court – there were cottages there. I was born in 1901 in Charlton Vale near the White Horse pub where there were three little cottages, real country ones, and some stalls and stables belonging to Swaffews the greengrocers. You entered from the gasworks and the road came out at the soup kitchen by the river. There were gangs down there, fellows from the Rope Yard Rails – a tough lot. Then there was Coonices' Barge Yard, Tuxford barges which was full of slate and bricks, thousands of 'em. Near there were some dockyard gates. It was said the prisoners had marched to work through there to the hulks and that's where folk used to slip them baccy or a bit of grub if they could spare it, sometimes even clothes if a local felt sorry for one, for they needed the clothes to disguise themselves if they were going to hook it, or so our grandads told us anyway. They marched in over the main Woolwich Road under the gateway in the churchyard to the boats. Back from there was Trinity Street, called Warspite Road now, and at the bottom of that was the *Warspite*, a big old iron-sider which was used for training boy sailors; perhaps they were orphans, but they were a cheeky lot none the less.

The original *Warspite* had been towed away to Greenhithe in 1901, but another training ship replaced her, and the name stuck.

Harry Thomas Harris recalls the *Warspite*: "Below the coal derricks where the colliers unloaded in all that dust was the training ship *Warspite*, an old wooden wall. When we passed her in the evening the lads on her deck would semaphore to us with their arms, this causing loud laughter amongst them." What the messages were remain unrecorded, but according to Grandad they were invariably unprintable. Uncle Con, Grandad's second son, remembers,

> These little blighters would save up their trash you see – old food, all kind of rubbish, and they'd wait for Grandad to scull under the *Warspite* and the lot would come down on his head – the air went blue every time some poor bloke in his dish got pelted.
>
> Then of course, there was Siemen's, a German firm, which led to a few punch-ups in the First World War. There was then a track, it never had a name, and Castle Shipbreakers, where all the figureheads were lined up, and all the old masts were floated for they kept hoping sail would come back and they could use them again; lots of the old boys thought it was just a matter of time before they built sail again. The *Cutty Sark* lay rotting for years near there – there's one they saved at least . . . Hardens Manor Way was by Charlton Bank, then there was a field, and Vasey's barge builders who had it both ways. They used to build lighters and break 'em up. Then there was Howlett's, they built them too, then Garratt's Yard, then the wharves where the guano and nut ships moored and unloaded – locust beans, peanuts in shells which went over the river to make margarine in the big works at Silvertown, and tiger nuts, then there was the Key Jetty Paint Works, and the Anchor & Hope pub.

The Anchor & Hope was an old riverside tavern, and its name derived from the days when sailing barges and brigs came to Charlton to load ballast. In those days, adverse weather would often mean a skipper had to spend days waiting for the right wind to get out again, and so he 'anchored and hoped.' It was virtually the 'village hall' and focal point for all festivities. The racing skiffs for the watermen's races would be launched there and past races discussed whilst the proud possessors of Doggett's Coat and Badge medals

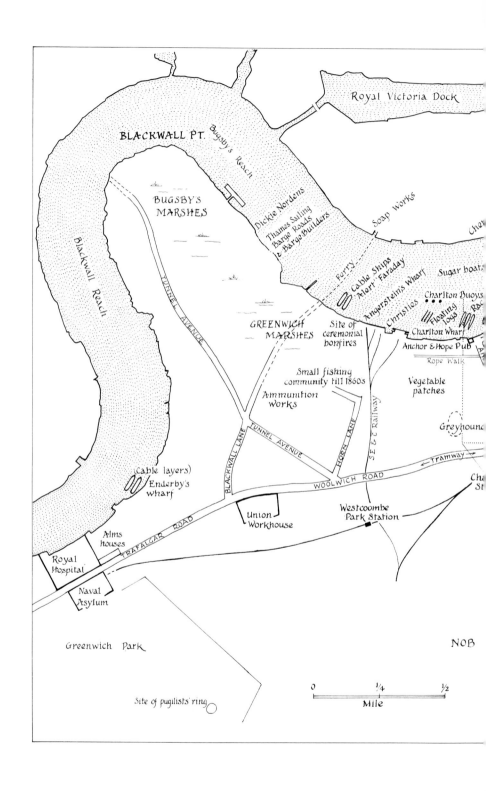

Royal Victoria Dock

BLACKWALL PT.

Bugsby's Reach

BUGSBY'S
MARSHES

Blackwall Reach

Dickie Nordens

Thames Sailing
Barge Roads
& Barge Builders

Soap works

Che

Ferry

Cable Ships
Alert 'Faraday'

Angerstein's Wharf

Christies

Sugar boats

Charlton Buoys

Floating
logs

Ra

GREENWICH
MARSHES

Site of
ceremonial
bonfires

Charlton Wharf

Anchor & Hope Pub

A

Rope Walk

TUNNEL AVENUE

Small fishing
community till 1860s

Vegetable
patches

Ammunition
Works

HORN LANE

SE & C Railway

Greyhound

BLACKWALL LANE

TUNNEL AVENUE

Tramway

(Cable layers)
Enderby's
wharf

WOOLWICH ROAD

Cha
St

Westcoombe
Park Station

Union
Workhouse

Alms
houses

TRAFALGAR ROAD

Royal
Hospital

Naval
Asylum

Greenwich Park

NOB

Site of pugilists' ring

0   ¼   ½
Mile

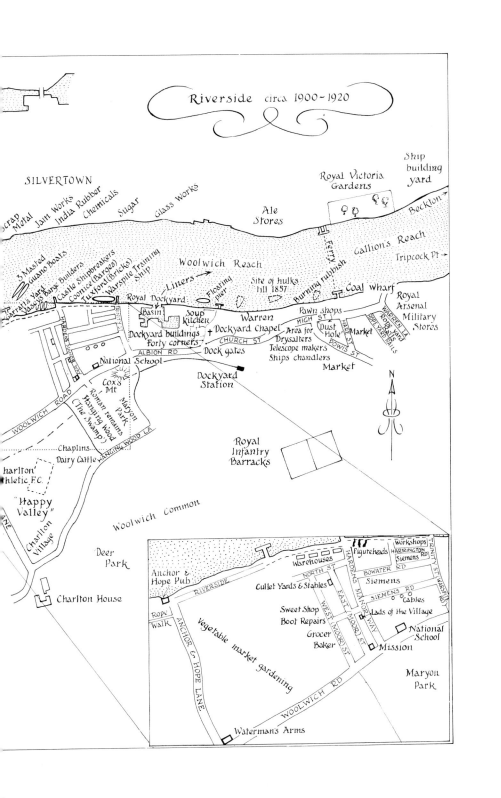

Riverside circa 1900~1920

SILVERTOWN

Scrap Metal
Jam Works
India Rubber
Chemicals
Sugar
Glass Works

Ale Stores

Royal Victoria Gardens

Ship building yard

Beckton →

3 Masted Guano Boats
Varrah's Yard
Vasey's Barge Builders
Castle Shipbreakers
Cornice (barges)
Tuxford (bricks)
Warspite Training Ship

Woolwich Reach

Galion's Reach

Tripcock Pt →

Liners
Floating pier
Site of hulks till 1857
Burning rubbish
Ferry
Coal Wharf

Royal Dockyard
Basin
Soup kitchen
Dockyard buildings
Forty corners
Dockyard Chapel
Warren
Pawn shops
HIGH ST
Area for Drysalters
Telescope makers
Ships chandlers
Dust Hole
HARE ST
WARREN LANE
ROPE YARD RAILS
Market
POWIS ST
Market

Royal Arsenal Military Stores

CHURCH ST
Dock gates
ALBION RD
National School

N

Cox's Mt
Maryon Park
Roman remains
Hanging Wood ("The Swamp")
HANGING WOOD LA

Dockyard Station

Chaplins
Dairy Cattle

Charlton Athletic F.C.

"Happy Valley"

WOOLWICH ROAD

Charlton Village

Woolwich Common

Deer Park

Royal Infantry Barracks

Charlton House

Anchor & Hope Pub

RIVERSIDE

Rope Walk

ANCHOR & HOPE LANE

Vegetable market gardening

Warehouses
Cullet Yards & Stables
Sweet Shop
Boot Repairs
Grocer
Baker

NORTH ST
HARDENS MANOR RD
WEST MOOR ST
EAST MOOR ST

Figureheads
Siemens
BOWATER RD
Siemens
SIEMENS RD
Cables
Lads of the Village
Mission

Workshops
HARRINGTON RD
Siemens
TRINITY ST (WARSPITE RD)

National School

Maryon Park

WOOLWICH RD

Waterman's Arms

allowed the odd favoured neighbourhood kid to finger the fine metalwork with its horse of Hanover, and gape at the collection of pictures and cuttings which once adorned the walls. Bob Sargent recalled when he and his large family had lived there:

It's been in my family since 1858. We were all watermen. There are three clans of us, all related way back; there's one here on the Thames, another at Gravesend, and another on the Medway. Some have been Trinity House pilots, and for generations we have all been Freemen of Watermen's Hall. There were ten of us. All of us provided pilots upriver, ferried lightermen, tied up vessels to buoys – everything in that direction. Our H.Q. used to be an old barge called *The Frances*. Lovely old thing she was. Then we moved downriver half a mile to Hardens Manor Way, and I sold her for fifty-one pounds to a bloke who wanted to make her into a houseboat. Gawd knows how he got her downriver in one piece. The old Anchor and Hope was always alive, what with ten of us, and each year the greasy pole game, the launchings and brass bands.

Charlie Jackson continued his imaginary walk down the Riverside from the Anchor and Hope: "If you walked on, you came to Charlton Wharf, near Rope Walk, and then A. H. Corey's. Off here was Charlton Buoys where the sugar was unloaded for Tate & Lyle. The Lads of the Village was their local. Royals they were, got good money like the guano-boat men."

Mr. Steatham who wrote to me from his house in Eltham was a lighterman who had worked off Charlton Buoys and recalled the stevedores here: "I must mention the sugar ships which moored at Charlton Buoys. They were manned by stevedores, local and from over the water. These stevedores used to rig the derricks themselves and discharge overboard into lighters perhaps 10,000 tons of raw sugar in two hundredweight sacks. Without hardly looking they'd swing these heavy things and stow them perfectly, then they'd go and sink their pints at the Lads of the Village; they took real pride in this skill."

Along the river, the smell of raw sugar would give way to that of creosote and timber as one neared Christie's yard with its piles of telegraph poles, and then an open space of marshland with small allotments of cabbages and rhubarb before Angerstein's Wharf where the South East and Chatham Railway line cut through the Greenwich marshes. Further on was Enderby's Wharf where the great cable-laying ships stood, crewed by Charlton men, many of whom had perished in 1874 when *La Plata* sailed from New Charlton with a crew of ninety-five, 183 nautical miles of heavy cable and 219 tons of coal, making her heavily overladen in the stern. On that occasion the ship had been hit by a storm, and Coxswain Lamont had survived four days in a life-raft in the Gulf Stream of the Bay of Biscay. He had been picked up by a Dutch schooner, and had kept himself alive, ironically, by sucking his medal from the Ship-wrecked Fishermen and Mariners' Society to ward off his thirst, but sixty-eight local crewmen never returned. It was not unnatural then, that the departure of a cable-ship for her long duty was attended by a good turnout, as Mr. Steatham explains: "The cable ship *Dominion* was a big beauty, and she would lay off-shore at Enderby's Wharf taking in miles of cable for weeks before her sailing day, and when that day arrived the word went round 'The *Dominion*'s sailing!' and crowds of people would run along the river bank from their homes cheering like mad as she pulled away. There were lots of local men in her, you see."

When things had described a bit of a slump in 1907, Grandad had signed on the *Faraday* as a cableman, but the work hadn't suited him enough to stay. He signed off six weeks later and went back to the barges, short takings notwithstanding.

At Dickie Norden's on the marshes, the sailing bargemen would collect in the hopes of a freight, and the barges would lay in Bugsby's Reach, where the schooner *Enford* unloaded bricks, while Edmonds the builders hammered at new barges in Point Wharf, and their rivals, Pearmines, at the marshes hurried to complete a new lighter. The little watermen's village had disappeared behind a gasworks, and their tiny Kentish cottages were cut through by the Millwall extension line crowded with dock-labourers to Millwall Junction and the docks. Along Horn Lane, where more watermen had lived in isolation, stood the ammunition works, soon to employ thousands of over-the-water people in the Great War's expansion, and the Union Workhouse in Calvert Road was still opening its doors. This then was the scene around the four streets, and beyond it the river full of sights for a young kid to gawk at.

Mr. Steatham again: "I would run to Lovell's Wharf at the sound of the Cunarders, *Alaunia* or *Antonia*. These lovely deep sirens sent a shiver down your back to watch them as they steamed up Blackwall Reach with two spotless 'Sun' tugs at their head. Later I was bound to a master as an apprentice lighterman on a big steam tug called *Enid*

Blanche but I never lost the tingling sensation at those sirens; the sound went right through you."

And if the sight of the liners palled as they worked into the Outer Basin from Canada, or South Africa and America, there were the huge cargo vessels to watch as the Blue Stars, laden with meat, or the Jamaica Stars with bananas, worked into the Royal Albert, and you could excitedly try and guess what Uncle Fred had brought from Capetown for you. If the wind was in your direction, you knew the guano boat was in wherever you were. Or you could just stand and watch the sailing barges working up on a bad neap tide, which, if there was a strong westerly wind as well "was really something – to see them tack, zig-zagging from one side of the river to the other, trying to make a little headway, whilst the boy winched the lee-boards and trimmed sail".

The neighbourhood was going through hard times at the turn of the century. Queen Victoria had died in 1901, and though folk whispered, it was hoped for a King with a more humorous side to his nature, the vast majority of people only remembering the sombre old lady in her latter years and widow's weeds. Unemployment was rife and the Arsenal was laying off men by the score. Many hundreds had been encouraged to pack their bags and move to the new plants in Greenock, and the coronation of the new King Edward also heralded marches of unemployed men through the streets, and filled Rope Yard Rail Alms houses. This was the era of Jesse Collins' 'Back to the Land' policy, and enticing encouragements were made to return to 'three acres and a cow', but the preceding years had broken the last rural links for the people the scheme was encouraging, and it failed. 1903 had seen an explosion at the Arsenal when thirty-three had been killed, and the streets around Charlton were full of unemployed men, many of them Boer War veterans, some perhaps still favouring the low crowned bowlers of thirty years before, as they knelt in East Street playing skittles in the gutter, or pitch and toss when the law wasn't about. In 1911 and 1912 we must have come desperately close to the kind of unrest which was seething in Russia, for with the strikes on the docks and railways, there were 3,000 troops posted in Hyde Park, 4,000 in Battersea and 3,000 in Regents Park with heavy reinforcements at Woolwich.

It was a hideously hot summer in 1912 and little knots of people stood around, some still seething that 150 dock strikers led by local Harry Hart had not been allowed by the chaplain to pass the hat round at a special service, and King George V was advised to postpone his intended visit to cut the first sod for the new dock extension. Woolwich Tunnel opened to put more ferrymen out of a job. Then just over a fortnight before someone took a pot shot at the Archduke Ferdinand in a place called Sarajevo which nobody had ever heard of, tenants in the little houses skirting the waterfront of North Street were brought hurrying to their doors by the screech of iron plate grinding against iron plate and hiss of boilers as the steamer *Oriole* and the liner *Corinthian* collided with each other off the Anchor and Hope. *Oriole* was sinking fast, and *Corinthian* had a hole in her bow which you could have driven a 'knifeboard' horsebus through. Bob Sargent's father and one of his brothers leapt into their best wherry, the *Nancy*, and rowed out to the listing *Corinthian* whilst blankets were unrolled and tea brewed for the survivors in a dozen houses along North Street. The little *Nancy* – a finely varnished wherry which had been passed down through the Sargent family and now resides in Greenwich Maritime Museum representing an age when watermen polished their boats till you could see your face in them – safely landed sixteen people. Another local waterman, George Kennaird, rowed madly downriver with a hurricane lamp in an effort to stop the *Golden Eagle* ferry which was thrashing her way up, and he successfully managed to avert the sort of disaster which had befallen *Princess Alice* years before. While the *Oriole* wallowed over on her side like a dead whale off the Anchor & Hope, the people of Riverside can be excused for saving only those cuttings about her from the *Daily Mirror* of June 8th, and discarding the other pages which warned of the huge fleet Germany was building. Twenty days later, the First World War was triggered.

This, then, was the atmosphere from which most of the living memories started. Suddenly everyone with a normal complement of fingers was in work, and those with Teutonic-sounding names crossed theirs, as the *Kentish Independent* exhorted people to retain their friendly feelings towards those German workers at Siemen's who had not been repatriated. Suddenly the docks were inundated with vessels which had been diverted from French and Belgian ports, and the dockers doubled their numbers from about 4,000 to 8,000 workers. The Dreadnought shipyards upriver, which had been started by a redundant lighterman at the turn of the century, were heavy with the sounds of riveting, and sailormen were finding that they could earn a year's salary in a fortnight, sailing the Channel

The Daily Mirror

LATEST CERTIFIED CIRCULATION MORE THAN **940,000** COPIES PER DAY

No. 3,314.   Registered at the G.P.O. as a Newspaper.   MONDAY, JUNE 8, 1914   One Halfpenny.

EXCITING RESCUES FROM STEAMER SUNK IN THE THAMES: PLUCKY WATERMEN WHO WERE INSTRUMENTAL IN SAVING MANY LIVES.

Hole driven in the Corinthian's bow

The Oriole lying on her port side. The picture was taken looking towards the vessel's stern.

Waterman Joseph Sargent and his young son William.

Captain Dale, of the Oriole.

Waterman George Kennaird

One of the Oriole's lifeboats smashed in the collision.

There were some thrilling rescue scenes near Greenwich on Saturday following a collision between the steamer Oriole and the liner Corinthian. Though the former vessel sank in a few minutes, no lives were lost. Great pluck and resource were shown by two Thames watermen named Kennaird and Sargent. With his son, Sargent rowed out to the scene and saved sixteen lives, while Kennaird, knowing that the Golden Eagle was due, seized a hurricane lamp, and pulling up stream as hard as he could was able to warn the vessel. Otherwise she would, in all probability, have crashed into the wreck which was lying right across the fairway.—(*Daily Mirror* photographs.)

with pitch, coal and armaments for the Front with the same kind of unhurried deliberation as in peacetime. Occasionally a U-boat would surface to capture a crew, or in the case of the *Ivernia* in 1914, her skipper woke up to find himself staring into the face of a German destroyer lieutenant with a boarding party, and spent the rest of the war in internment along with many others who had been caught well up the Rhine when war was declared, or tarried too long in Antwerp taking off refugees.

All these adventurous escapades still had the romance of a Balaclava or Omdurman to the young boys who listened by the R.A.S.C. Band playing in the Arsenal, and it was natural that they should be swept up in the wild fervour which led to voluntary regiments such as 'The Footballing Enthusiasts Battalion', and 'The Optimists Corps' made up of lightermen. Posters exhorted 'Come on Boys – don't wait to be pushed!' My Aunt Ann with other bright-eyed girls cheered Australian soldiers in their wide-brimmed hats marching along Hanging Wood Lane, and Thames sailing barges and lighters found themselves as far afield as the Tigris and Gallipoli.

Women workers at Woolwich Arsenal during the First World War, loading the TNT.

Hoch der Kaiser was a street Arab's joke that went with newspaper hats and wooden guns. It was in this enthusiasm that both upriver and downriver boys who could add a few months to their ages slipped out of school, as in the case of Charlie Jackson:

There were sixteen of us kids in North Street but only four survived the war. I played truant a lot, and in 1915 I ran away for several months. I went down to Dickie Norden's in my long trews and told him I'd left school, so I was taken on as cook boy on the *Scud*. Your grandad worked that one, too. We went off to Beckton to pick up coke and continued over to Calais. You could walk the length of the East Dock there on barges, one after another; it was crammed with them, all loading with freight for the Front. I came back for another trip after laying over there for a month, and arrived at Bugsby's Hole for a paint up. When we arrived, old man Norden says to my skipper, Teddy Brown, "I got two gents wants to see yer boy". He called me Bobby then. "You're wanted in the office, two pots." "Yesser," says I.

These two gents are waiting when I gets in, and my heart's thumping like the clappers. We'd just been through a war zone, and it's only here my heart starts thumping. "Are you Bobby Jackson?" says one. I can't say a thing. "Right then," says he. "You come along with us – I'm the School Board man and this is a policeman, and you're going back to school for the two days until you are fourteen and can legally leave."

I went back to Maryon Park School, and knocks on the headmaster's door. His name was Gates, and he had a swipe like a heavyweight. He just looks up at me standing there and says, "You didn't oughta run away until you're fourteen. You must stay for the rest of today, but here's two and sixpence, and the best of luck." You could have knocked me down with a feather! I went back to Dickie Norden's, legal this time, and spent the next two years with skipper Brooks on the *Glenmore* when we were running from Lambeth with empty barrels down to Totnes in Devon for cider. The Whiteways factory stood on that empty site by Vauxhall Bridge.

Mrs. Nellie Shakels, in her little house in Battersea, gave me some idea of the boom in work at this time above bridge. Her father, James Taylor, was a fourth generation lighterman.

My dad had started work at twelve. He'd always wanted to be a lighter-man like his father, although he had drowned, but we were proud of Grandad's Doggett's Coat and Badge which he'd won. It had been presented by Prince Albert but now it's in New Zealand, for some of our family emigrated there years ago. Anyway, there was masses of work in the First World War. Dad would leave our home in Surrey Lane by the river's edge, at about four thirty a.m. and be in the pub by Aldgate Tube at five a.m. which had a special licence to open at that time. Breakfast was a tot of rum to keep out the cold, and the work was called on there. Sometimes he'd sleep under canvas on one of the lighters over there. He was sweeping down supplies to London Docks, everything from uniforms to food, and it would be loaded up for the Front. Funny thing was, he could never swim. You'd think that with Grandad drowning he'd learn, but one night, about 1916, he comes home dripping wet. He'd sat on the number 12 tram like that. He'd fallen in, and a lady had taken him into her house, and said: "You can't go home like that." He was smelly too – in the wharfsides it was pretty slimy. "I got no option, dear," he says. Anyway, she gives him a nice cup of tea, says her husband's away at the Front, and all she's got is his overcoat; hasn't got no trousers, she says. Anyway, he comes home on the number 12 tram wearing this overcoat and her bloomers! You didn't dare laugh, though – he was a tough one. And having nothing but daughters in the family, one brother had ten, didn't help his humour any. He was a close sort of man, and though later he was attached to the R.A.S.C. and was involved in some action, he never said a word about it, just "There's nothing to it", he'd say.

Well downriver, too, lads who might otherwise have thought of other professions, had forgotten the pre-war slump, and signed on, like Captain Bertie Fry, whom I visited next in his small house in Greenhithe, a little corner of Kent where there is still a colony of retired sailormen and sailmakers.

I went to sea when I was thirteen and a half on the *Beatrice Maud*. My father was skipper. We were running across to the Continent with pitch and coal from Blackwall Ridge and Queensborough to Calais, Boulogne, Ostend and Dieppe. There were some schooners doing it too, some of them carrying explosives. They always congregated off the Lower Hope, loading from an I.C.I. vessel but we gave them a wide berth. They were long runs, and we took no extra hands. There was no such thing as a system of watches, you kipped where you could. I was a sort of cabin boy serving my apprenticeship for Watermen's Hall with my half-indenture and I was on the hop the whole time, tacking, winching, cooking, and when I wasn't doing that I was polishing something.

In 1914 just after I'd started, the Germans shelled Scarborough lighthouse, and we felt a bit uneasy. Suddenly the Channel seemed very narrow, and sometimes you passed a vessel which could have been a friend or an enemy, half the time you just didn't know, what with the Q ships as well. They were rigged up to look like innocent trawlers or merchantmen, and they'd have a great gun hidden under hatches which could be run out in minutes and blast you out of the water.

The sailorman is an independent cuss, and we rather resented the Royal Navy bossing us about; there was never any love lost there. It was not unusual for sailormen to cheer as a fleet of fast boats shot round East Anglia with guns roaring. They'd heave to to watch the battle, and then read in the newspapers that they'd been Jerries. It was all very mixed up. Then there were the Naval cutters – Dad couldn't stand them blokes. These examination boats would come alongside, Royal Naval jobs, wanted to know your name, your job, what socks you were wearing. They treated everybody like spies. I remember once, we're off Broad-stairs, and up comes this drifter, a two-ringer [lieutenant] with his megaphone, and Dad, who was a proper old sailorman if you catch my meaning, had had just about enough for we'd been examined twice already.

"Where are you from?" bawls this two-ringer.

So and so.

"Where are you bound?"

So and so.

"What is your cargo?"

So and so.

"When did you leave?"

So and so.

All the time we're trying to hold her steady. This two-ringer is evidently trying out his anti-spy routine and gets cute.

"Where were you born?"

"Hoo."

"You!"

"Hoo!"

"YOU!"

'Course, he was born in Hoo.

Another time, there wasn't a hair's breath of wind, along comes this Naval cutter.

"Heave your vessel to."

There's no wind you see, so we didn't do anything. Hell, there wasn't anything *to* do!

"Are you going to heave your vessel to?" And then, "If you don't heave your vessel to, I'll put a shot across your bows."

We was standing still, no wind you see, and the old man says, "What the bloody hell are we supposed to do?" The mate suggests, "Let's go and put the bowline on." That's to bring the foresail across the ship like a brake. Anyway we do this, then the two-ringer is happy. We wasn't going through the water at all – the bob looked like a dead sock! No, they didn't know how to handle pure sail, and of course, there was the class thing, too.

It was a source of some amusement to two or at the most, four-handed coasting bargemen to hear of the *Sarah Colebrooke* which had been commissioned by the Royal Navy in 1917, and renamed H.M.S. *Bolham* who now carried four officers, three engineers, two wireless operators, three petty officers, several signalmen and ratings all crammed into her one hundred and two feet six inch length. Her lee-board was heavily reinforced, and in her Q-ship role, she finally came across a U-boat. *Bolham* fired, and the submarine appeared to sink. Once in dock she was attended with great ceremony by top brass from the Admiralty, and her commander was awarded the D.S.C. The U-boat, however, was sighted some weeks later showing no sign of damage, but it's not recorded whether the lieutenant had to give his medal back.

Naturally enough, the sailorman in his solitary barge was unaware of a greater pattern, if any pattern existed as far as the Naval Command went. But it was a fact that many barges were kept waiting off Southend for weeks at a time, and at least one skipper resorted to deliberately sailing into mine-fields in order to be towed off by the Navy in the hopes of getting his long-awaited clearance, without which he could not get his freight delivered and mate paid off. Again, in that congestion, where vessels waited without lights for clearance, it was bound to happen that Naval patrol boats collided with bargemen, as in the case of *Centaur* which was hit by a patrol boat. At this time too, a shadow of the hulks returned – this time to Southend Pier, where several vessels were at anchor filled with enemy aliens.

Enemy planes firing over Erith in 1914 brought the war home to people on the riverside for the first time, along with black-out routines, although the moonlit Thames shining like a snail's thread up to the docks was a perfect navigation line. The first Zeppelins came over in May 1915, and Charlton and Woolwich underwent some six attacks before ground defences could even scratch them. On September 2nd, 1916, crowds in the streets cheered Lt. Robinson in his fragile biplane as he shot down the S11 at Cuffley. From then on, every Zeppelin was said to have been shot down by a 'Robinson'.

In June 1917 the Albert Docks were badly damaged with 200 people killed in the City. Later, planes began raids. The crew of the *John Evelyn* were killed instantly whilst berthed at London Docks when an incendiary dropped straight through the skylight, and on June 13th, 1917, eighteen small children were killed in Poplar (there's a memorial in St. Mathias Road).

In the three years between May 1915 and May 1918, riverside wives and children had stories to tell their menfolk when they returned from what had hitherto been a distant war.

Bertie Fry's wife, was born and brought up in London's riverside, and remembers the excitement of being a child when a Zeppelin went over:

> They'd go over, huge things, always looked as if they were sliding sideways, and occasionally you'd hear this sort of droning noise, then the searchlights would pick it up, and it would hover there like a huge cigar. 'Course, we were supposed to be under cover, but you couldn't help standing in the back garden to watch it. We saw the first one come down over Billericay way, but my sister leaps up into the air, and so I never saw anything else because, silly thing, she'd dropped her purse, and there we were on our hands and knees looking for pennies. But we could hear people cheering. After, somebody would pedal round on their bike shouting "All clear!" and all the kids would rush out looking for pieces of shrapnel.

Nothing could dampen a waterman's sense of humour, however, and 'Buster' Keaton, a local man who had been drafted into the Arsenal Army, wrote in a 1918 newspaper:

> We were ordered to take up positions at the back of the gun park. The night was very dark and raining hard as we were going along Ha ha Road. As we neared our gun position Jerry was getting the best of the argument . . . we were expecting to feel the smack of a bullet any minute as they were falling thick and fast all round us. We were in a fine pickle, and I had had enough of it when my pal from Rope Yard Rails said suddenly: "I don't care much for this lark!" "What's wrong wiv yer now?" I said. "Get a move on or we'll be high high up in the hills watching the clouds roll by." "Oh, all right," he said, "but I wish I had me muvver-in-law here now. She'd be able to liven things up."

As if the enemy contribution wasn't enough, the Silvertown works where explosives were chemically refined opposite Charlton blew up in January 1917. The whole area was cordoned off, and the only escape was via water; fleets of wherries and everything floatable ferried survivors over the river to the four streets, and once again, blankets were broken out and that universal panacea, tea, was brewed. However, the interval between fire breaking out and the subsequent explosion, proved a death-trap. Many people were caught in a ring of fire, and the inhabitants of North, West and East Street stood impotently watching the holocaust which set the river a vivid red colour. Sixty people were killed, and 400 made homeless, and when most of them were receiving only the one and a penny a day, with an extra sixpence severance pay and twopence for each child under fourteen for husbands away at the Front, destitution was not far round the corner for those made homeless.

That same year Bertie Fry was mate in the *Marjorie* with his father above bridge. Charlie Jackson had gone over to the barges which were carrying cement to Gravesend Reach and Chatham, where the *Swiftsure* was being prepared as a Zeebrugge blockade ship.

"One time we were with sixty-two barges at anchor off Deal – some for Dieppe and some for Calais – all loaded with coke, and we heard that German U-boats were about and had captured several crews. It was an uneasy feeling for we all remembered Jackie Joss who'd been snatched off the *Ivernia*. I remember him coming home – he looked awful."

The end of the war arrived, and armies of men returned hoping to pick up where they had left off. Charlie Jackson was in Antwerp when peace was declared, and has less cause to remember the declaration than suddenly finding himself with a skipper who had over-indulged, and a return home which was a little less than glorious.

I was on the *Emily Jane* in Antwerp. There was also the *Beatrice Maud* and the *British Lion*. We were all loaded with pitch, and when peace was declared, we got stuck there; so long that the pitch had set like a ballroom floor and we had to chip the blinking stuff out. We applied for some freight, and the *John and Sara*, *Beatrice Maud* and *British Lion* were loaded with pit-props for the Humber; the *British Lion* was for London, and we for Middlesbrough. We all left together, with a pilot for the first bit. It was very decent weather, and we came off the Ramikins, off Flushing. All the mates went ashore there on the sandbanks as there were fine cockles about. My old skipper who was seventy-five we called 'Line' Tommy Scott 'cause he'd tell a line and believe it himself. He had a

Pomeranian dog with him, and no less than twelve canaries down the scuttleway. I slept in the forecastle, thank God. His missus was with us as mate all through the war; she'd been a Sunday School mistress, but by the time Tommy'd got through she wasn't no prude. Anyway, they all started to puff up like balloons. So much for our week's holiday, the first I'd ever had, as they'd got cockle-poisoning, and were laid out. I didn't know what to do. I shouted that my skipper had taken ill, and I was told to follow *Beatrice Maud* and *British Lion*. "But I'm only the boy, I ain't experienced in this!" I called. "You follow us, you'll be all right." I was at the wheel for thirty-six hours until we made Harwich. The skipper was okay by then so I made him and his missus a cup of tea. I was walking dead, and all he said was, "You'll do . . ." So I went home.

After the war a Q-ship, the Suffolk Coast, *lying in St. Katharine's dock and the U-boat, U 155, lying alongside her.*

11

Friends and Neighbours

Tis a snug little house I reside in,
And the people who're living next door,
Are smothered completely such pride in,
As I ain't never met with before:
But outside the door they don't roam
For a 'uge sum of money they owe a-body,
If folks call they can't find them at home,
But I never says nothing to nobody.

Music Hall Song 1906

THE WAR FINISHED and the neighbourhood got down to the expected 'better things'. People tried to forget the years of rationing and public meal orders which had stipulated 'two meatless days a week', and the hay-box oven was thrown on the compost heap. However, just as had happened after the Napoleonic War, the Boer War and many other conflicts, thousands found themselves out of work. The dock expansion scheme was continued, and some found employment digging the George V dock. Though when Manor Way disappeared under several tons of water, and a sudden barrage of high walls and police patrols barred the way, it was a backhanded benefit to riversiders who had had the right of access to the river front before. In 1920, disabled Servicemen who had been promised secure work at the Arsenal were dismissed, and the fat went straight into the fire. Eleven thousand riversiders, many of them ex-servicemen who felt they'd earned a bit of jam on their bread, were stopped at Westminster Bridge where the Riot Act was read, and an hour-long pitched battle with the police ensued. In 1921, several councillors in Poplar were arrested for refusing to levy rates, and by 1923, ex-soldiers and sailors were marching through the streets proclaiming 'Is this the Land for Heroes?' and even the more sober Civil Service marched with them, with '3,000 Ex-Service Civil-Service sacked – 26,000 non-service retained.'

However, political events were way above the heads of the youngsters in Riverside who were probably more taken with the new white lines which appeared on roads for the first time in 1924. Against the backdrop of slumps and the general strike, my father and his brothers and sisters grew up, unaware, except for the odd immediate incident, of the wider pressures which were now on their older mates' shoulders. So before hearing of life and work aboard the barges after the war that was supposed to have ended all wars, I decided to try and open a few doors of those now-gone houses, and

The ships came clear to the houses, Mills & Knight's dock, Bermondsey Wall, 1924.

put a face to some of the occupants whose nicknames had filtered through Grandad's front parlour door of a Sunday tea when old times were discussed.

Charlie Jackson was tightening his belt:

"After the war, things got a bit slack – I spent days up at the City looking for work. Thirty shillings didn't go far then and my last wages were soon used up by the time I'd paid Mum her share for the family. You asked around the broker's offices in Fenchurch Street, round there. Worked for a bit on a schooner, *Enford*, usually bricks, then I shipped out on the *Mary B. Mitchell*. She'd been a Q-ship during the war, had all the notices inside her and was supposed to have sunk four German subs. They were mostly Irish in the crew so they took me for my London river knowhow. I was eighteen months with her, then it would be the same round, walking Fenchurch Street, then round to Goldsmith's at Greys to see lines of barges doing nothing. Skippers at Starvation Dock nearby were selling them up fast, in some cases their whole livelihood sold for £15. Each night back home – nothing, but there was always good mates who would give you their last halfpenny if they had it.

There'd be loads of kids hanging about the gates of Siemen's saying, "Got any overs, Guv?" 'Overs' were scraps of lunch left. Oh, the kids still played, but it was a hungry time. Each Monday Mum would put my best suit in pawn and have it out again for Sunday best – all the families did that.

Bob Sargeant was a strikebound apprentice in 1926, indentured to his mother who had taken over the Anchor & Hope. (His father had seen the war end, but had died in the 'flu epidemic of 1918.) "I was fourteen, and the strikers pelted us with rocks from the bridges upriver – actually we weren't scabbing – but it was terrifying. I was only a kid."

And Nellie Shakels recalls a hint of wider implications: "People stood around in knots, mumbling. Nobody seemed to laugh. One day I was standing at Battersea Bridge Road, and a bloke came along on a motor bike. He skidded and the bike went over, he sprawled over the street, and as he fell a revolver slid out of his pocket at my feet. That was the first time I was really scared."

One day in 1926 a petrol lorry tried to break the picket line at Charlton pier, my Uncle Con was there:

This petrol lorry came down trying to break the picket lines. It had the old solid tyres, and strikers were hacking at it trying to break the fuel pipes; there was petrol everywhere. Suddenly someone called "Here's the police." They were from up London, specials, and therefore had no emotional links with us locals. They came roaring down in one of those open police wagons like the Keystone Cops. As they passed, a lad behind me must have picked up a stone from the rhubarb fields and hurled it at the police wagon. It hit the driver. Suddenly the thing went out of control and coppers were sent sprawling in all directions. They were really mad, and started slogging out at everybody with long truncheons. Anyway, things got out of hand and everybody fled in panic and slammed their doors shut. Grandad, who hadn't been involved at all, was on his way home, and Auntie Ann just managed to get him through the door; he was hit several times, though. They wanted this kid's hide. Anyway, there was a three-masted guano boat at Charlton buoys being worked by stevedores, all local men, so the boy was smuggled on her, and for all I know he got himself off on a two year cruise, 'cause they never got him. But they were bad times.

Dad tried hard, but it wasn't easy feeding us lot, and whilst we were honest, there were times when desperation dictated what you did. You didn't enjoy it, but again I can remember being sent down the road to get some bread with a sixpence, and I'd try and nift one, so as I could then buy some best eating apples with the tanner and stuff them on the way home. But strangely, some of our favourite dishes came from those times. A bloke would come round the streets selling speckled fruit, that's to say it was too far gone to sell to posher people, but we'd hash them up in batter and fry them. They were delicious, and bananas the same way, fried in suet or batter. Funny thing, you wandered round for days dreaming of food!

However, as with so many events, it was a case of your own circumstances dictating your point of view, for upriver Winston Churchill was declaring that the dockers and lightermen were causing 'criminal obstructions . . . to starve the people and wreck the state'. One hundred and five lorries of Grenadier Guards and armoured cars of the Royal Tank Corps were drafted to dockland, and newspapers feted the 150 students and middle-class volunteers who had brought lighters towed by an owner down from Westminster Pier to Victoria Docks to break the strike. Submarines sneaked out carcasses of meat to the coastal storage plants. The strike ended. The younger kids no doubt bemoaned the fact that the soldiers with their shiny fixed bayonets had gone, and the neighbourhood got on with the business of living.

1926. Many hands make heavy work as student volunteers unload food supplies at Hays Wharf on the seventh day of the General Strike.

Uncle Con, as an older boy, was expected to pay his share:

Every pay-day all the workmen used to play a game called 'Upsy-ansoms'. They'd put two halfpennies on their thumbs and flick them up, betting on the result. It was an adaptation of 'Pitch and Toss' and there'd be money all over the ground. It was my job to keep the two and sixpence which they'd whipped round to collect, and watch at the corner for the copper. When he arrived, he'd look up to the sky and shove his hand out as he passed mumbling, "Thank you, son . . ." Between number 12 and 28 was Welsh's cullet yards – old Mother Garlick's son had a truck with tyres, but most of the cullet was fetched on carts, going round all the breweries collecting the glass and sorting it into colours; it was big business. We were bare-footed then, and could leap around on all those piles of glass without cutting our feet; it was the odd bit on a hard pavement which did the damage.

Those cullet yards were a scream sometimes. Old Mother Garlick's house backed on to ours, and she had Tate & Lyle sacks up at the window. She was always saying, "My, I really must get some new curtains." But even if they were sacks, they were always washed and clean although she just couldn't get the maker's name out . . . She wasn't much at feeding her son though, every week was a comedy. Her house had this long passage running down to the scullery; the door was always open, and he'd shout down "You got me lunch, Mum?" . . . "There y'ar, Jimmy." He'd open it, and it'd be dry bread; he used to throw it right down the passage 'Bonk!' it went, never missed!

What I liked best was cleaning all the horses' tack on Sundays. I'd get sixpence for that. One was a retired American radio horse from the war; one day I sat on it just to get the feel, and it reared up, I smashed my head on a beam and saw the stars and stripes for ever all right! But I loved those horses; there were fifty of them, and they would just let themselves be unhitched and walk into their own stalls. One had pink eyes, and nobody could handle it but me. I used to help the blacksmith there too; it was wonderful to watch him hammering out those wheel spokes so true. One day a horse kicked him in the face, and he was never the same again. But it was so warm by the forge – December 19th, 1927 was the coldest day for thirty-two years. Another way I earned a bit, was looking after the lightermen's barges when they were at lunch. Or I'd watch the wherries – some of them were licensed for fourteen passengers, and they'd come back, some of them very happy and I'd find myself rowing twenty of them back to work with the boat about two inches above water – but I got a shilling for that.

Charlie Jackson remembers other ways to make ends meet:

The Fosters, Tarrants, Summerfields, Jack Allstock – we'd all earn a few bob now and then working for the Sargent brothers. But there were some characters – there was Loopy Thomas a few doors down who used to run along Riverside in a white sheet trying to scare courting couples till one night someone tripped him over; mad as a hatter he was. Then there was Kosher Goodman in Manor Way – he was one of the best footballers Charlton ever had, then Jim and Lotty Waites at 68 – he became a boxer and it was said he was also a film extra and banged the Rank gong, and then the Jays – they were the greyhound experts and the Lees, a real rustic family. Poor old 'Mother No-nose' had a grey porcelain nose tied on with tape round the back of her head; you couldn't take your eyes off it. Then the Swales at 40, we could never make them out, they were gypsies, I think. Anyway, little Jimmy Swales was about four feet tall and was always sitting on the wall in a bowler hat. He always had a broken clay pipe stuck in his mouth, and he'd ask, "Got a light, George?" every time people passed. 'Got a light', I don't think he ever bought a box of matches in his life. John Garrett and John T. lived at 138 and 140, they were barge builders and breakers, then the Kings at 90. The Keys, Downs and Bowers were all watermen, and the Montagues who had their own barges. Then there were the Manchesters who also owned horses, and an old boy, a cabby; he always wore a bowler, had this old horse which looked as if it would drop dead any minute – we called it 'Fire Engine'. We'd whistle and that thing would bolt like a greyhound out of the slips with him swearing at us. But we never had much time for cabbies – it was a traditional thing.

The shops were marvellous places; the goods would be all in sacks and barrels, not packeted up, and you'd get the smell of beans, tea, coffee; it would make your stomach rumble. At number 17 West Street, was Mrs. Richards, the 'Sweet'; she used to make her own toffee and lay it out in the window with little stickers saying ½d and a ¼d. We'd sneak in and change the stickers round but she always knew. She had this parrot which used to scream "Mum, he's pinchin the sweets!" as soon as you went in. I can remember once going in and buying a gobstopper. There were high steps in the front door and I tripped down them and swallowed the gobstopper; it stuck in my throat and I had to sit in the kerb waiting for it to melt for ages – what annoyed me most was that I couldn't taste it. Lodders' was another shop – beautiful bulls' eyes, and liquorice, hundreds and thousands, Spanish strips, and Jap desserts, a sort of caramel. The best value was the sticky bits left in the bottoms of all the jars – and toffees – except that they were wrapped in newspaper and you had to eat that, too. You got a heap for a farthing.

I can remember the streets clearly – there were so many characters. In North Street where I lived there were the Doughtys and the Carters; they were at 31, two doors down from us, and they were a tough lot. You didn't get on the wrong side of Carter who went on to bigger things, if you catch my meaning. His mum had a stall up the market – she was a tough one, too. At 53 West Street lived Frank Grusker with Harry, Bill, Em, Violet and Alice – I was related to them. One uncle way back had been hung for stealing a sheep off the Kent Marshes. William Dixon at 87 was a lighterman. Then there was Old Mother Mags and her donkey who sold firewood, Joe Brean's cabbage patch, Kingy the butcher, and Wheeler the bloke who came round with his donkey selling ice-cream. I remember Mr. Welshman's donkey, too – it dropped dead right outside the Prince of Wales pub. I can remember the local copper, his name was Warby, 'Bluebottle' we called him. He never pinched anybody – he'd just take them down to the Silica works, take off his jacket and give them a good hiding; he never made it official, just the ditch, and a good pasting. Even Carter and Doughty learned not to mess his patch up! The Oglers [river police], were the same; they were all watermen, our kind you know, and they'd sweep past in their galleys and the worst you got was a smack round the ear.

However the area was split into 'manors' and boys were in gangs. My uncle elaborated:

First of all, Woolwich Road might have been the Brandenburg Gate. My wife, as is now, lived over the other side, and was never allowed to cross the road to the Waterman's Arms area. All the boys over her side wore school uniforms and neat little caps. They never walked past us, they *sped* past. There were gangs, split into territories and pub areas, that's to say the forecourts, were neutral areas. A call would go out that the Wallace Street Gang were approaching, and every boy over eight ran into the house to grab the old lady's copper stick. I was a West Street boy.

Most of the kids were just high spirited, but there were gangs of older boys round Rope Yard Rails who were a tough lot; most of them earned a living by filching and foraging, from mudlarking to stealing where they could, but we were all right – we had Harry Carter. But we observed rules – girls were never involved, and a feud would be settled by an organised battle, but never in the streets or round our homes, and vandalism was rare. Cox's Mount was the battle ground, and we'd congregate there at the prescribed time and await 'the enemy'. I can remember once, we were waiting there, bricks and copper sticks at the ready but the opposing gang hadn't turned up, then they appeared like a row of Indians up on the Mount. A signal was shouted, and all hell broke loose: there's a railway nearby with a signal box, and the signalman came out to ask us to stop and everybody turned on him; nobody touched him, but his signal box looked like Crystal Palace after the fire, with every pane broken. However, he should not have interfered for it was the way things were settled here, and we never bloodied anyone's nose who had not elected to join the party. Nor was there any mugging at night.

Strange as it seems to say, there was a code, and honour meant something then. I can remember once, this code was broken, and it showed me that older men like Grandad had been shaped by the same way of doing things. Everybody belted kids then, but to correct, not to cause injury. I can remember once brother Ted came home with a black eye. Viney the boxer down the road had done it – he was much older and therefore considered 'a man'. A swipe round the backside would have been all right, but a black eye . . . Dad had his jacket off in a minute and marched

She (concluding the argument). "AN' IF YOU WANT TO DO YER NEIGHBOURS A GOOD TURN, GO AN' THROW YER 'AT IN THE RIVER—AN' DON'T LET GO OF IT."

off down the street, doors opening all the way down, but Viney had got wind and disappeared.

We started school at three or four years old then. It was free there [Maryon Park], but it cost threepence a week at the National School. I can remember my first day for I was wearing my first pair of clogs. Eightpence a pair, they were. It was a strict school, lines on the playground, and when the whistle blew you froze. Old Gates was handy with the switch. I remember getting one right across the veins of the wrist once for pulling the wings off a fly which had walked across my book, not for killing the fly mind you, but for not paying attention. It was mostly the three R's, and we learned by imitation, that's why everybody of my generation writes with a neat sloping hand; it's the way you had to write, letters forward, and neatly looped.

It was the time of the Government health drives in schools. One day you'd line up and have your tonsils out, another day there was 'Nitty Nora' searching everybody's hair with the same comb, then another time a bloke came to say we had to go and be tested for specs – there were piles of them – little wire things that curled round the ears. They put this sign up with letters you'd need a magnifying glass to read, then said, "Yes, you need spectacles." It was the funniest sight, all those kids in clogs reeling around staring out of spectacles. I can remember walking home and the ground was coming up at me – couldn't see a thing. I threw them over a hedge. What a racket! I knew chaps who stuck to those glasses, and now they're half blind; I've never needed them to this day. Someone was making a fortune. The intentions were good, but you can't heal people on an assembly line. Then there were so many more children in the streets with rickets and who'd had polio. It was a common thing to see a boy or girl in leg irons, usually with bare feet. Anyway, school was from nine till four thirty, and then after all the chores were done riverside was our oyster.

Back gardens, apart from being a cacophony of chickens and ducks, also housed the Kentish passion for pigeon racing, and their little coops, rabbit hutches and chicken runs were interspersed with makeshift kennels, which housed the other object of Charlton Riverside passions, the greyhounds. A working man's fancy stretching as far as Lancashire, and the Jays of North Street were the accredited experts in this field. Hounds were raced on a small patch of cleared shrubland near Rope Walk, and here of a Saturday, enthusiastic locals would lay their bets in the grass, whilst strategically-placed children watched out for the law.

In 1903 the East Street Mission just round the corner had initiated a weekly football match on the meadow near Siemen's, and the little mission which had been designed to keep so many of the footloose youngsters out of Maidstone Assizes was adopted by a public school. The 'Charlton Reds', as they were called, had worn out the grass after a few wild games, and the 'Addicks' had to transport their rough goalposts over to Woolwich Common. Then, as Charlton Athletic and top of Division Two, they had begged, borrowed or stolen a better pitch in Pound Park down Hanging Wood Lane which the kids had dubbed 'the swamp'. These fields belonged to Benson the butcher, who pastured his stock in the lush grass there. When Deptford power station was built, the rubble was hauled over to build a conventional ground. Charlton Athletic, teamed by local lads, was attended by enthusiasts from all over the wrong side of Woolwich Road who sprawled in the grass of a Saturday afternoon, with their stone bottles of ginger beer and tiger nuts to cheer on what was very much a home team. Kosher Goodman's back garden of number 50 would be a bright display of eleven home-made red shirts dripping from the copper on a Monday noon.

If the West Street Gang were feeling particularly doughty, they might sneak out of their own territory, and climb carefully on the roofs of the Arsenal store-rooms in Manor Way over to the large Naval practice targets on the marshes, where they could gain a good view of the opposition at the Arsenal football ground. In fact the Arsenal itself was a great playground. Beyond the Arsenal buildings was an area known emotively as 'danger ground', a wide marsh running along the river, broken only by a few huts, three-feet-high walking areas and special tracklines to transport munition workers to their work. If watchmen caught any of them round Mugby Junction, they got chased off, but the fishing was good. There were also the mysteries of the slate slab in the mortuary nearby, and the more fastidious girls could pick the spring crocuses that grew along the bank or wave from 'T' Pier at the *Golden Eagle* ferry, on which Bob Sargent's uncle worked, on its way to Southend.

Towards evening when the prices fell sharply, there was Woolwich market, its uneven cobblestones bright with naphtha lights over a hundred stalls. Here in the 20s, in addition to fruit, vegetables, cut-price sweets, fish, meat and sausages, there was a whole host of gratis entertainment. There were Red-Indian medicine men with accents suspiciously reminiscent of the Elephant and Castle who would draw your teeth or cure your warts for a bob. There was Abbott's Wonder Soap which apparently cured ring-worm. A man selling writing paper announced out of the corner of his mouth that it was "shipwrecked stock, and flowed into our privy last night". Comic salesmen who had wagon loads of *Magnet, Hotspur* and *Girl's Crystal* told you to 'jerk off' when they saw you trying to read them at the stall, and the hot potato man might be there with his circular boiler if it was cold, or the hokey-pokey man if it was hot. There was the 'lino king' smacking his yard-stick on the oilcloth and drowning out the cries of 'toffee mac', and 'Mr. Gibson the razor king', and a large knot of people round Spittalhouse's chippie. The 'purse king' would be vying for trade with Sid's china stall where real 'boney' was hurled over the heads of the assembled crowd to a would-be buyer, whilst his accomplice kept up a breathless sales patter. This was still the age of the street ballad seller with his farthing copies of *Firty Fahsand Pounds* and *The Council Schools are Good Enough For me*, and on the odd corner sat modellers in clay, glass painters, tattooists and barbers, their customers squatting on the kerbstone. If you searched diligently you might even find someone with that most bizarre of highly prized trophies, a caul, for sale. The birth of a baby with this membrane over its face was an occasion for jubilation, for when dried and worn in a little pouch round the neck, the caul which had protected the unborn baby in the watery womb was supposed to save sailors from drowning. A 1779 newspaper advertisement of one for sale states: 'Enquire at Bartlett's Buildings Coffee House, Holborn. NB To avoid unnecessary trouble, the price is 20 gns.' Purchases of this rather gory item are in fact recorded as late as 1944, and I suspect that the custom has only really died out because more and more babies are born in hospitals.

However, to the inhabitants of West Street, the market meant the meat auction on a Saturday night. Large job-lots would be held aloft, and it was the girls' duty to pick up a good Sunday joint whilst the boys just went along for the ride, or in the hopes of seeing a good punch-up near the pubs where the pathetic prostitutes of The Dust Hole near the Garrison picked up their clients. The stock answer to "Who wants a leg of lamb for half-a-crown?" was, "If you'll wrap it in two breasts I'll have it!" "Three penn'orth of steak pieces to fry," would go to augment the Sunday feast of boiled bacon which was usually cured at home by elder sisters on Saturday afternoon. Let Uncle Con remember Saturday nights:

I always remember Saturday nights at home. None of the houses on our side could afford proper gas mantles, we'd just use the fish tails as the unprotected mantles were called, so at night you looked out on dozens of naked flames flaring in people's windows. We had two bedrooms, three of us in bed with Dad when he was ashore, and Uncle Ernie, the youngest, slept in a box. The two girls slept in the other bedroom. The house was so old the wall bulged over the bed-head and there was a big crack in it. I used to lay there having nightmares of falling into the street.

Every Sunday morning we'd wake up to 'The Laughing Policeman' blaring down the street. It was Harry Woodman, he did it deliberately; he had one of those old 'His Master's Voice' horn gramophones, and 'cause he always got up early, he'd wind it up, open the window and play the thing to the street. Anyway, he got his 'come-uppance'. His chimney needed sweeping badly for his old mum was a cripple, and needed a fire most of the time. He was always collecting firewood down at Castle Ship-breakers where of course it was covered in pitch, and you'd hear her saying, "Harry, that's too high . . . Harry, don't stoke it up any more, we'll have the chimney alight." One day it was. Nearly had the whole street down. We never had any more 'Laughing Policeman'.

We had no bathroom, and there was only one tap in the scullery – with four boys you can imagine the fights over the sink. I used to wait for Charlie or Ted to start scrapping in the garden, and I'd nip in and wash down while they were scrapping out there. I remember once the old man's rose-arch got smashed. Roses were his passion so all hell broke loose that day.

After the Sunday blow-out, the costers appeared around four p.m. with red herrings, winkles, whelks and oysters. The muffin man with his bell and a tray on his head was another regular. Front doors would open hurriedly to queue for the 'Kempton pie man' as he set up his primus stove by the kerb-stones. Street games abounded. Hoops and tops of course, five-stones and marbles, two-balls (and 'three-balls' for the experts) against the front wall, and queke (or the medieval game of hop-scotch which represented the Trinity). Curious crazes seemed to sweep the 20s, a dafter one each year. There was an eight-sided top which you spun to gain a score, which-ever side fell uppermost. This was an adaptation of the middle-class *'Ca ne fait rien'* (It doesn't matter), but down here it was 'San Faryan'. There were pogo sticks, put and take, and tee-toe-tum.

"I used to make balls from the rubber bands round the broken cullet – you know, those broken bottle necks which had india-rubber sealing bands round them. The balls were never completely round and you never knew where they'd bounce. Many's the time I've hidden in the lavatory because I'd busted a sixpenny window!"

However, it was to the river the children graduated, no doubt to the horror of many bargemen who lived in their own vessels between the breaker's yards and Vaseys, for their little chimneys stuck up from the cuddies at a tantalising eye level, and were a constant temptation to children who had endured rigorous school discipline all week. A favourite pastime was to stuff old rags down them and then watch from a convenient distance when the choking skipper and his mate came out for air. Then there were lines of lighters, some of them partially submerged:

We used to learn to swim in them, all amongst the skipjacks, and of course we could fish off them, for eels mostly, and the odd mullet. It's strange that parts of the river here were as clear as glass. I never knew of a kid getting sick from pollution; over the other side, where the chemicals were, yes, but not on the Charlton side. Some kids were good divers and could earn quite a bit bringing up the odd piece of copper; rope fetched a bit too, and bolts which we sold to builders. Where the ships were unloaded for the margarine factories almost at the bottom of our street was a wall of masts sometimes. The odd sack spilled open as the scoop swung across the water, and this was a source of sweets to us kids. Tiger nuts and locust beans are hard, shrivelled little things in the barrels, but when they'd been in the water for a few hours, they swelled up and split like pop-corn – with the salt in the water they were delicious. I don't think waterside Londoners will ever forget the taste of them.

Your dad was younger than me, and I always had to look after him. There were always younger ones trailing on the arms of older boys in those days, the families were so big. I can remember once we were imitating the lumbermen at Garratt's Yard, there were great floating masts there from the old windjammers, your dad slipped between the gap and they closed over his head. We all went mad, for kids were always drowning that way. The oglers had seen us, and were heading over to help when I see your dad's head sticking out like a moving football, he was just walking along the bottom; that's how clear the water must have been for him to look up and find his way beyond the mastheads into clearer water. Occasionally you'd see an old boy with his trim tram net out there, flinging it over his head and spreading it over the water with a flick of the wrist.

One of the boys owned his own bike too and he'd let it out to us at twopence an hour. I used to pedal down Riverside with it making the devil of a row for it had no tyres, till I met this Bobby – an ogler he was, though you never associated them with legs. I hit him and he sprawled over the bank and into the water. I turned the bike round and pedalled away as fast as I could, didn't stop to look round. But they'd know the poor kid who owned the bike for not many people had them. It must have looked comical sometimes when occasionally up on the main road you'd get the bike wheel caught in the tram line, and with no brakes you hung on for dear life hoping you wouldn't meet a tram on the same tracks.

We did range for miles, mostly over the marshes where you could find good mushrooms. Occasionally we went over Greenwich Park and up through Westcombe Park; a lot of the wives and daughters from the Lower Woolwich Road were in service up in those big houses, but not round our way, for being a servant was a blow to pride in the four streets. I remember once going to Greenwich Palace pushing your dad in a wheel-barrow. The streets were uneven then with huge wooden blocks; I'd slipped and fallen and the wheelbarrow had overturned and your dad was all soot-stained and tearful. We peered in through the railings at all the columns and passages, at the huge three-masted Dreadnought there, and we waited for the King to come out 'cos we thought it was Buckingham Palace.

Actually, there is a rational explanation to this belief, because of course, Greenwich had been a palace, and there were family stories of Grandad having seen the King there, and very much in mufti at that. The King and Queen had a small son, Prince John, who was born in 1905. The poor kid was unstable and worse, it showed. Where better to install such a child than in the enclosed area of Greenwich Palace under the quiet supervision of a seconded sailor where he might occasionally break loose and pull faces through the railings as people passed along Park Row? A reported sighting might have been discussed by Grandad with a mate, and overheard by the boys, who then also wanted to go and see the King. The newspapers of January 18th, 1919 kept a low profile in announcing the death of 'Prince John, youngest son . . . who was rarely seen on State Occasions . . .'

Memories of Christmas are especially strong on the waterfront, even though next day, a man might scull out to a barge road with no inkling of where his next freight was coming from, or how long he could hold out. Doors would be open all down the street, and hoarded pennies were taken down from the jam jar on the mantel-piece. Whatever was to happen, the kids should have a good time – it was the same all along the riverside and indeed throughout the working classes.

> The older people, those who were still very Victorian, [according to Charlie Jackson] would decorate their hearths with hundreds of pictures of the King, the Queen, Union Jacks, rosettes, ribbons and witch-balls – the mantelpiece would be covered in them. Every window would have a small Christmas tree, and old stockings would be filled – always with an apple, an orange, some nuts and a brand new penny – it had to be new and unused – it was traditional. The copper was a talisman against crimple-ham.

And in return the kids, with some inkling of the dwindling family resources, might attempt the odd small gesture as a Christmas Box. Uncle Con again:

> Grandad had a shed at the bottom of the yard, and one day all his tools had gone. I see your dad's head down there, kept poking out looking round and disappearing again. I thought, what's he up to keep popping in and out? He was in there for hours. Dad comes home to mend some-thing. "Where's my saw? . . . Where's my hammer? . . . Who's got my

chisel?" I said, "It's not me, it's Charlie." He gets a clout and starts to cry. It comes out he's been polishing all the tools as a Christmas present, so then I get a clout for telling tales, for that'd touched his heart you see . . . In the scullery the Christmas pudding would be taken down from where it had hung in muslin for a year for you always made your pud for the following year to season it. All the families would visit each other, one after the other, and the invitation at the door was "Come in and muck yourself." Now they'd think you meant something rude.

It was the same off Odell's Barge Yard in Battersea for Nellie Shakels.

The beds of our two rooms would be pushed in a row, and we'd sit there facing each other. It was everybody's duty to sing a song or tell a poem in turn. We went down the row, and several people could play penny whistles or concertinas. Some of the songs were a bit rude:

Cover it over quick Jemima,
The dogs are after me bubble and squeak,
Cover it over quick!

or there would be the odd song like those my dad sang.

There was father half undressed,
Lying in the gutter with the mangle on his chest,
Half in the middle of the road!

Everybody could relate to those songs, as evictions were quite common. It was one of my jobs to keep an eye out for the rent man. As he got to the door, I'd go out and say, "Mum says she's not in!" Those were things you had to make a joke about or go barmy.

And the sailorman would laugh along with the rest, to please the kids. For there was precious little time to enjoy the riverside before they grew up and at fourteen had to wake up to the realities of 1928.

Woolwich Free Ferry John Benn *seen from the North Woolwich bank c. 1923.*

12

Dead 'uns and Downalong

The verdict was that too much wet
This poor young woman died on:
For she made an 'ole in the River Thames
What the penny-steamers ride on.
                              'The Rat-Catcher's Daughter'

WHILST THE INTERVALS between paying off and signing on grew longer, brokers' offices became more crowded with skippers, and the lines of empty barges in their roads at Woolwich Buoys, Bugsby's and Starvation Dock waited there that bit longer in the natural slackening which followed the 'big dollar' days of the First World War. The sailing barge traffic was still in its heyday in the 20s, the threat of the motorised Dutchman and the trucking fleets were just a rather ominous gleam in a few businessmen's eyes and wouldn't really pose a crippling threat until the early thirties. Yet the sailorman's living was a precarious one, depending as it did on the weather, and if there was a big north easterly round the Nore, and you happened to be making for Blackwater, you just had to ride it out at Southend and wait. There was no such thing as hourly pay. The traditional process was one half to the owner, two thirds of the remainder to the skipper and one third for the mate. Inevitably, a crew often squared up in debt. A wry letter home might run, "Dear Muvver: I'm sending you two pound this week. One in ballast, one in sugar . . ."

In the days when the absence of a favourable wind meant the difference between breaking even and being just plain broke, there were dozens of superstitions to appeal to. Many sailormen would whistle down the wind, or the odd hair thrown in the water was a small investment. The London Scots believed firmly in scratching on the mast to summon up a blow.

Bertie Fry summed up the latterday sailorman's feelings about the old superstitions: "We were not superstitious, or 'simplicious' as the western bargeman would say, to any fanatical degree, but we knew Providence was about there somewhere, and we had little insurances here and there; what your father did, you did sort of thing. We didn't laugh at the old Bonsors' beliefs. I suppose you'd say we couldn't prove it wrong, so we didn't knock it." As old as the hills was the technique of 'buying' the wind, and many vessels sailed with a coin hidden inside the mast – in fact many were constructed with a coin inside the tabernacle box. Dick Virgo and Captain Goodwin testified to this belief:

> Buying the wind – I've seen it work too many times to doubt it. If you were becalmed, you asked the sky for wind. You'd say, "What's your price?" Then throw a halfpenny over the side. It always worked. As a young shaver I was a bit sceptical, and I recall one time I was taking the *Louise* for a refit. We were becalmed – not a hair's breath of wind. I see the skipper of *Magnet* buy his wind – he's not a hundred yards away from me, but he pays, and off he sweeps into Pegwell Bay, and I'm still stuck there – not a hair's breath. I've never doubted it since.

It was a 'mizzling mulligrubber' indeed who could not thrill to the moment when open waters were reached, and where as Dickens recalled, 'the festooned sails might fly out to the wind', and apprentices like Bertie Fry, Dick Virgo and Charlie Jackson inherited their unique know-how. As the river widened from Erith sands along the wild Saxon shore to the open sea the sailorman came into his element, making use of the natural system of swatchways as a motorist might read signposts, and Bertie Fry recalls:

> We didn't use charts sailing. If somebody took a stone off the beach we knew it. We knew the way of the tides because that was our living . . . where it went strongest, slack tides where the tides go off the bights, and good tides. It was shifting all the time. Up off East Anglia when I was a boy there were dozens of masts, ships . . . God knows how old they were

. . . all those masts sticking up out of the water. The sands would shift; sometimes it was hard enough to play football on, the next minute it was sucking everything down; what the Essex bargeman would call 'quackling'. I reckon there's the history of sail under those sands, not to mention hidden villages, West Rocks, Orwell, Cork Sand and the Naze Flats. Walton on the Naze was still called by some old fellows by its ancient name 'Eadulfesness' or 'Adululnasa'. Take Northfleet Ho for example and St. Clement's Reach; you learned under sail to let nature gentle you along. On the south side the craft were head up for an ebb-tide, the other half, flood; there's the eddy you see?

The tides in the Thames now, the ebb or flood goes round all bights [curves], the slack waters are round the points, like round my elbow, back, slack, bend, tide. So if you got the slack tide you were stuck. When there was a favourable wind, you tacked, tacked, tacked all the time like a flirty old lady in crinolines showing her bustle, one side then the other. The marvellous thing about it was, there were hardly no collisions; it fascinates even me, for the river at that time of day was as busy as a High Street in the rush hour. You had boat days when there were queues of them for the Port of London. I've seen Long Reach between Purfleet and Grays, coming up from St. Clement's at night – hundreds of them. All we had was a tail light, those at port and starboard and no mast lights. There were steam boats, flat irons, liners, merchantmen – Janes' *All the World Shipping* – like a damn game of draughts, but we could read them.

Here then was the 'shop-floor' where a man would choose to work in preference to the grunting steam yards of Blackwell. The river bends down to Erith on the gravel beds where centuries of barges have ballasted, and Tilbury which was once a heavily defended fortress, where at World's End pub watermen have met and swopped stories for years. The Lower Hope offered some shelter from Sea Reach where the strong sea currents take over, cutting the coasts of Kent and Essex into dozens of small inlets and islands, Canvey, Grain, Stoke Saltings, Burntwick, Sheppey, Elmley, Fowley, Hasty. Uncompromisingly functional names crop up like Mucking Flats, and Hole Haven, or the sombre Dead Man's Island lying off Tailness Marsh and Shepherd's Creek, where bodies of cholera victims from the prison hulks had been buried during the Napoleonic War. Here Bertie Fry had his first encounter with 'a dead 'un' – one of many which the tides took on to inlets all down the Thames and Medway.

When I was just a slip of a lad, we used to put into Swaleness. It was a

A barge builder's wharf at Conyer, Kent, 1936.

dismal place, and I used to look out at Dead Man's Island, and go ashore there with my hair standing on end. You could see the shape of the coffins in the mud, and I could never take my mind off what was underneath those shapes; what with the wind howling and birds screaming overhead, it was eerie. They'd been dug in years before and been well inland then. I used to dream of the sea eroding them further and know that one day I'd find one. It was part of your graduation to find, and get over finding, a dead 'un, but you never ate shrimps once you'd seen one.

My time came as it's come to all sailormen one stage or another when I must have been about sixteen. We came out of a mud-hole, and there wasn't a hair's breath of wind in the heavens. I was mate to the old man then. We were laid in the mud-hole, loaded and waiting to float out, and so off I went to collect some driftwood for the fire with my sack on my back. Low water tide. I'm walking along the edge of the marsh. The tide's about sixty feet out. I picked a bit of wood up, I see something floating, I can't make out what it is. I don't go down. Just at that time a fish-cutter went by, the waves from it rolling in, and this thing turns over. It was a feller with a bald head . . . I done no more! I shot back, I leaped ditches, what have you. I jumped inboard. It was a lovely day and my old man's lying asleep against the headboard.

"What the bloody hell's the matter with you?"

I said, "There's a dead 'un out there, Dad! There's a dead 'un!"

"Bloody fool!" he said. "He won't hurt you!"

That was that. That night there still wasn't a hair's breath of wind in the heaven, so we have to long boom out, push it out on poles. We're just coming out the entrance of the mud-hole, I throw my boom, for the old chap's on the other side with the other boom, and I see it again.

"There 'e goes, Dad – there 'e goes!"

"Push on that bloody boom," says the old man. "Never mind about 'im – he won't bite yer!"

We get outside and let go the anchor. Next morning, low tide, we're making sail. I said, "There 'e is again, Dad!"

The old man says, "Who?"

"On the edge of the water there," I says. (I hadn't slept a wink thinking of this bald man floating about there, thinking every lapping sound is that head of his against the hull.)

"Come on!" he says.

"What for?" I says.

"We're going to 'ave a look!" he says.

"Here – No! . . . hang on!" I says. "I don't want to look at 'im!"

Anyway, he would insist on my having a look. We sculled up, and well . . . He had shrimps coming out of his eyes, his mouth, nose – I can't tell yer! So I says, "What are we going to do about him, Dad?"

"Nothing," says Dad. "He's all right where he is."

We couldn't afford to stop working. Tide and Time . . . Anyhow, he was picked up later, came from Manor Way. I never got used to it, though – even later, much later.

Anyway, that was one of the muckier lessons, but from Dad I learned the ways of the marshes. He caught eels the old way, with the three-pronged spear in the ditch, but we had other ways. I used to collect lug-worms from the mud, and thread them on to a piece of worsted – like a necklace, then tie it together on a stick, and sit back in the boat with it just in the water. You'd feel him come on, and then pull him in. The eel's teeth are like little hooks, and once he's bitten, he can't let go till his tail touches something like the bottom of your boat. Then he'd jump off and you had him. Allhallows was a good place for 'dabbing' or 'bumming'. It was back-aching, but you didn't worry about things like that. You moved along in about a foot of water, with your hands flat on the sand, and you could feel the fish under your palm. Dad told me, that if ever you tried it, the first one you would never catch, because when you put your hand over the fish, a plaice or flounder, his tail would whip up under yer wrist and you let go.

Time was when Dad got more for his fish than his freight after half had gone to the owner and one third of the rest to his mate. He used to trawl occasionally on the way to Johnson's at Greenhithe with cement. He'd sell his catch there – we only got by with that sometimes. Oh, the owner upkept the barge, but you had to supply your own food. Nanny would make it up for me in watertight bags, but if you were laid up in bad weather, it was a dead loss, you needed to find food elsewhere – but shrimps, no! Nor winkles for the same reason, though most ate them. And I suppose other things got took at times – who was to see anyhow?

For Charlie Jackson, January 1928 saw the terrible floods which hit the upper reaches of the Thames, and a temporary spell off the barges:

I'd been walking around for days, the odd job for a few weeks ballasting and cement. Then I served on *The Navaho*. She was the biggest thing I've ever seen; she wasn't unlike a huge barge, or barque – six masts, six sails – over 6,000 tons. She only had a small auxiliary engine, and belonged to the Anglo American Oil Company of New Orleans, Baton Rouge and Tampico. The men were signed on as sailors, not as able-bodied seamen, and I went as bosun. We were towed downriver and then canvas took her. I did one trip in her, then she was sold to the Finns. A marvellous craft she was, and she seemed to me the way things might be going, but her type wasn't developed at all. I think they threw the baby out with the bathwater when they scrapped her.

Through the following years, Bertie Fry carried a variety of freights in a variety of weathers:

You know the old saying, 'hard lines' – well, it meant just that. You look at any sailorman's hands, and he'll have a ridge running down the insides of all his fingers. It's scar tissue. Sometimes the frost was so sharp the sheets were like broom-handles through your palms, and you could never wear gloves, it was much too dangerous, but getting it through the blocks in cold weather was nobody's idea of a laugh, and your fingers split. We'd come home, let the cuts close up and hope that they'd be all right next trip.

I was mudding a lot in the 20s, then there was a bit of fodder and hay for the Tram Companies upalong. I only traded oysters once; funny it was, because it showed how people could stretch a point when it came to dollars. We were going to Brightlingsea with these oysters and we had adverse weather at Southend; we couldn't get down the swim, so we laid there at Southend for three days. We finally made Brightlingsea when the north-easterly had died down a bit with these oysters which were a bit round the corner by then. Mr. Stammers, who was from the Mussett people there, was a very religious man and I never thought he'd unload us on the Sabbath so I says, "See you Monday, then?" "Oh no, Cap'n," said he. "We'll unload now – we will unload to save life, otherwise them oysters will die."

The oyster people would come alongside with these boats like very flat punts, five or six feet wide like a floating box, heave the oysters out by hand winch, cut the basket open and shoot them out into wells, backwards and forwards, whilst we had a smoke and sunned ourselves. I don't suppose that's a sight which will come back. I can't say we didn't filch the odd oyster on the trip because we did.

Landfalls on the East Anglian coast were usually accompanied by the present of a bucket of herrings, which most crews hung overnight on lines, and as Captain Dick Virgo, who had gone to sea in 1923 with his wife as mate, and Mr. Godwin of the Crescent Shipping Co. told me, a delectable line of drying fish was fair game for poachers:

I always enjoyed those runs ashore for we were often given a present of fish, but when you'd hung them out you had to keep one eye open; it wasn't the sea-gulls you were watching so much as other skippers. I had this lovely cod once, and I come up in the morning just in time to see the *Alderman* passing, and there's the skipper standing aft holding up the fish with a big grin on his face; he'd swiped my bloody cod, and he was too far away to get hold of. We always ate suet the Suffolk way with jam or treacle before meat, never after. We also used to buy mutton by the yard, it was a penny halfpenny a pound then. The inside of the cuddy is dim lit, and as you cut it into strips, it shone with luminescence, but I never heard of anyone dying from it. [Meat in such a state was popularly believed to have aphrodisiac properties!] Another favourite was salt 'junk', bacon boiled for hours on a stove; the slight motion of the barge kept the salt-water moving. I think this was a universal dish with sailormen. We also 'dabbed', although round my way, we called it 'griping'.

All the skippers I spoke to were reticent on the subject of poaching, but clearly, mudding up deserted inlets offered a good opportunity for snares. As a child I can recall literally picking up a dozen small partridges walking along the marshland. Bertie Fry testifies to the stories of early camping days, when our family recalled seeing suspicious lanterns at night, and keel marks in Yantlet the next morning.

Certainly it was a temptation to poach, especially if the wind was no good and you were becalmed. Grandad carried a gun, and all those names which appear on the Kentish side, Mary Bay, Egypt Bay, Stangate Creek, there were blokes living there, especially in the village of Stoke which is about three miles inland over the marshes. It was a prosperous little village, but I never asked where they got their living from. Take Sheppey, you could land an army there then. Blackwater and the Crouch, Mersey Island, a boat timing himself across the channel, get there about two a.m., tide right, who'd know?

Certainly, there was the odd rogue skipper, as Charlie Jackson recalls:

Old 'Line' Tommy Scott, if he saw a likely customer at sea, say off Inner Dowsing, he'd send me over to the merchantman with a pound in my pocket. I'd scull over and up the Jacob's-ladder with the same old story:
"Please, sir, we've been becalmed for days, and run out of fresh grub. We're trying to make in to Harwich, but being weather-bound, we haven't had no fresh food for three days."

They were good blokes, and would give us a sack of fresh stuff. Never take anything for it, and I'd pocket the quid, but that was only him. Most of the time we were too busy to worry about fishing or messing about; it was hard enough to square up in profit, but all I'll say is, when we were away from London and in open country, we made the most of it, and weren't too popular up the Essex coast, especially with farmers.

However, people did have a sense of humour, nowhere more optimistic than on the river, and the following disastrous trip recalled by Charlie Jackson shows why a man had to have one or go barmy.

One February we were carrying Portland cement for Shrubshalls from Vauxhall. I think it was on the *Vicunia*. I was mate, my skipper was Jimmy Barker who had a terrible stutter. It was a nice passage up channel, and as we came round the long-nose buoy of Margate Roads, the weather closed in. We squared away and made fair wind. I was on the lead. It's four fathoms there – they called it 'The Overland Trail'. I'm calling – "three . . . three and a half." It was as black as pitch and Jimmy says, "All right, I think we're through, but take another dip."

So I swing the lead . . . "Three and a half . . . four fathoms, skipper, by the mark . . . hang on, it's three again . . ."

Jimmy is stuttering away trying to get out "We should be th . . . thr . . . th . . . th . . ." He's just got out 'through' when 'Bang!' we hit the black rock and she starts to fill up, there's a lot of compressed air at times, and she blew her hatches off like a gun. We managed to get off a flare, and *Reculver* must have spotted us, because some flares went up over Margate. We got in the dinghy, and eventually their boat came over to us and caught us in its searchlight. Jimmy was a plump little feller, and when we got to the lifeboat, he got halfway up and then got stuck in the rails – half in, half out with his backside stuck in my face. We all start pushing and pulling, and he finally shot through flat on his face on the deck. By this time we are helpless. Anyway, we're aboard the lifeboat and the coxswain, Parker his name was, is thinking he's picked up a bunch of idiots, and Jimmy's swearing, saying, "It ain't funny."

Anyway, they were good people at Margate, and they had this old taxi waiting for us; it was about one a.m. in the morning, and a filthy night, we're soaked to the skin, lost everything. Harry Parker said he'd put us up like, give us some rum and something to eat. We all climb into this taxi, in control now, and as we start away, 'Bang!' – the taxi gets a puncture. We were off again, filthy night, pouring with rain, and he says, "Will you push it for me?" So there we are, two shipwrecked sailormen, everything lost, and we're pushing this bloody taxi along Margate harbour at one o'clock in the morning, giggling like a bunch of maniacs from the looney bin. Jimmy says, "Here Harry – you forgot to weigh anchor," and Harry says "Bloody funny!" Anyway, we pushes the taxi all the way to Parker's house, and jump in a tub that his missus had put in front of the fire. Next morning, there's all new togs laid out for us, from some good fund or other; everything brand new, even the collar studs. We went back to London like two gents, nothing in our pockets and no shares – in fact we finished up owing them.

About four weeks later, I'm out with Ginger Pierce, we were on our way to fill up the *Sandrock* at Newhaven. We hit a heavy swell and waited for four hours under the cliffs, but we couldn't forget how much we owed, so we pushed out. The sea ripped off the weather lee-board. We brought her round, and off came the other one. There was only one thing, that was to go right across. Then the mainsail jammed. It was daylight, luckily, and the North Foreland saw our flares. A little vessel saw us in difficulties and tried to get a tow on us, and the sprit, bollards and all the sheets got ripped off. We were drifting on to the sands, and we couldn't use the boat because of the lee swell. Perhaps a breech buoy would work? They tried to come round us, to touch us on the bow, and we had to jump inboard; the boy lost his front teeth, my face was ripped by the wires and I lost most of my finger nails getting off. We were landed and days later heard a Dutch vessel had picked up our boat and towed her. But it wasn't funny that time. It was as if the sea was punishing us for not taking her seriously. It always seemed to be that way – first a hint of what she could do, and then if you didn't take the hint, she slapped you, and slapped you sharp. Under sail you always remembered that. I wonder sometimes whether these big oil-tankers with all their automation remember it, for she'll slap you sooner or later.

Many skippers combined this inland and coastal work, and after the war Bertie Fry, between worrying lay-offs, went further afield up to the Humber. The art of trimming a cargo was very important, particularly grain, as he explained: "We didn't load ourselves, only trimmed up, alongside a ship. You'd be called to 'hook on' by the shift-worker, and then you had to hook on and wait your turn coming alongside the grain hopper like an octopus. You laid alongside and trim under the wings by the mast; the art was in the trimming, a good skipper could get that much more in . . ."
Charlie recalls this knack too:

I used to go into Victoria quite a lot, with grain for McDougalls and the Co-op. It was crowded with lighters then. Perhaps occasionally I'd carry barley from Littlehampton, Yarmouth or Ipswich. Then again there'd be rough stuff, and there was an art in loading that up. You didn't do it yourself, but there's an art in going under sail alongside a dredger. You loaded in three heaps, and it was the way you loaded aft which was the study. You had to drop back amidships, and trim to the iron band. I had a busy time from the Iron Bight to Tilbury when they were building the dock gates there, sometimes four freights a week. We had a reputation amongst 'goozers' for being a bit grubby, our clothes and that, but they seemed to forget that they saw us at the end of a long, sleepless trip when our razors hadn't seen a strop for a week.

Bertie Fry recalled the same ballasting which Grandad had been engaged in.

It was a filthy job ballasting, especially if a load of grain came next because the whole thing had to be scrubbed out. I spent a lot of time carrying to the gangs building Thanet Way. That was largely built with roughstuff off the beaches at Brightlingsea. The beach there was dotted with beached barges. We'd sail in, ground, and then planks would be laid up against us, with lines of navvies with wheelbarrows loading backwards and forwards up these trestles. It was back-breaking work. Later they bought in a drag-line scoop, and we'd take it to Whitstable for the road building and more workmen would descend. From the air we must have looked like a lot of ants with the odd Queen which was the barge. Then I did the brickies. A lot of them were fired cullet; half the suburbs are living in glass houses. And then there was roughstuff from Wandsworth, all kinds of rubbish, come-what-may; we took that to Halstow where it was fired for bricks . . . funny that we should have been so eager to help build that blasted Thanet Way – a few years later it was finishing us with its fleets of lorries . . .

However, the writing was on the wall, and Captain Fry added sadly,

One time, I was reduced to carrying rubbish. I wouldn't have minded so much if she hadn't been a beautiful coaster. Anyhow, we picked this stuff up from Wandsworth to a small creek in the Medway; the stink by golly! Barges make water and you have to watch your pumps. When you'd had that stuff it came out black. It took about six months to get rid of that stink; it was everywhere, right in your bunk; you slept with it in your nostrils. There are no bulkheads. Sometimes you sat there of a night and looked at the table, and died a little bit with that smell. It was about that time I really knew I was on a loser, but I tried to keep going, hoping for better times.

All the length of the Thames and Medway, the story was becoming a dismal one. Les Williams wrote to me from his home in Sittingbourne:

> I'd started work in 1922, and had sat at my grandfather's feet just listening for hours for he'd been on the water since the age of ten, starting in fishing out of Harwich. In Sittingbourne then there must have been about 400 bargemen, all families on the water: the Aspins, Brooks, Spices, Wises, Shrubshalls, Cowards, Jemmetts and Reads, and they tended not to marry into each other. We had our own songs, 'Grace Darling', 'Pull for the Shore', 'Let the Lower Light keep burning' . . . There is talk of work-satisfaction and I've known very few jobs where I've had it, but by 1930 nobody wanted their boys to go on the water like their fathers and grandfathers.

Tom Sadler, a London lighterman apprenticed in 1922 noted the same fall-off:

> I was working on Australian fruit where the lighters had to be fumigated for insects, and then I became roadsman bosun looking after the roads of barges from my hut. By '30, a lot of the sailormen were changing to lighterage, and I used to sit there and notice that the lines of empty barges were getting longer. They were staying there for weeks more than they used to a few years before, and I also noticed that the sailormen were quieter then, there wasn't the old half-joke, half-insult blarney between us Londoners and the carrot-crunchers and chalkies.

Nanny Fry recalled the straw that broke the camel's back:

> We were getting poorer and poorer, what with three kids. Mrs. Gammin up the road, she went mate with her husband to save a bit; we went ballasting, mudding, and dredging coal for pennies. We'd lay off Gravesend for weeks, and, of course, we had to feed the mate, and then there was bad luck . . . I'd been put ashore at Gravesend with the children, when off Blackwall Ridge, our barge was cut almost in half by a Navy boat, the *Starling*. It was the crack of day, he came round the point, and hit us a real gutser on the starboard side. Daddy and the mate jumped into the boat and rowed ashore at Greenwich, and they woke up the A.P.C.C. Roads watchman in his little hut, and he gave them a couple of coats – me and Jack lost everything.
>
> And then there were the Dutch . . .

The Dutch incurred a good deal of bad feeling. It had always been there from the time when Dutch eel boats had enjoyed free moorings at Billingsgate. During the dock strike, Dutch blackleg labour had been brought over and now, with their motorised barges, they were posing a serious threat to the native barge trade. Dozens of Thames barges were hastily motorised, the delightful little cuddy being used for smelly engines, their skippers and crews being ousted from traditional living quarters to the forecastle, which caused many 'old bonzers' to give it all up in disgust.

But the problem went much deeper than where a man laid his head. The Dutch vessels were bigger and faster. A Thames sailing barge could take anything from four to fourteen days to reach the Port of London from Ipswich for example, so the faster Dutchman, carrying his family with him as supernumerary crew could undercut the wages of the Thames man. The Dutch needed no pilots, paid the same dues as English skippers, and furthermore received handsome subsidies from the Dutch Government as well as the 'Freedom of the Port of London' and 'Coastwise privilege'. English boats, by comparison, had to pay Dutch pilots and extra dues when in Hollandic waters, and had no rights to a return freight. The Dutch, furthermore, were adept at nosing out a freight wherever they went. They could often earn three pay-offs in one round trip by, for example, bringing up a load of perishable fruit to London, loading with grain for Felixstowe, returning to London with milled flour, then obtaining a freight back to Holland, and the average sailing barge company had no answer to this kind of enterprise. Some tried: J. R. Piper built rival 200 ton motor barges which could tow loaded lighters, and many companies went over to building motor vessels (sometimes commissioning continental builders like Papendricht of Holland – which did not cool tempers any), but they couldn't break the monopoly on the other side of the channel, nor could they undercut the wage bills.

This kind of competition was different to the coming of the railways when the little Margate Hoy Company had a whip-round and undercut the railway freight charges by a third. The Dutch were a foreign monopoly and the English were batting their heads up against a brick wall.

At every port and inlet the story was the same. Apart from the sailing barge the late 20s saw the end of several fine fishing fleets. Ramsgate had lost fifty of its 150 fleet in the First World War, and they'd never been replaced. By 1922 there were only twenty-five sailing smacks there, with thirty steam drifters, while by 1930 there were perhaps only 500 working sail-barges left. The 52,000 dockers of 1920 had been whittled down by mechanisation to almost half that number in 1930, so that men worked a 'stand-off' system by rotation.

The writer and artist John Lane, who left dozens of small silhouettes of the sail vessels surviving at the time, can perhaps be forgiven for assuming that the sailorman's state was a happy one. "At coastal ports to which the barges trade there are at the weekend in fine summer-time, hours to spare for deck repose and rest, so the ladies of the barge will rig awnings and produce deck-chairs, and secure in the privacy of an outer berth at a quayside, or unfrequented wharf, while away the time in pleasant talk, and it is agreeable to gaze upon such a spectacle." The fact that the sailorman and his missus probably had nothing else to do but 'while away' the time because they couldn't get a freight, doesn't seem to have occurred to him. He took some photographs of the ladies, followed by their addresses in Chatham for copies of the snaps, but the idyllic interlude seems to have come to a hasty end with the arrival of the skipper, "brawny arms attached to a six feet six inches frame", and Lane got on his bike and beat a hasty retreat.

Grandad threw in the towel as many Charlton men did, and crossed the road to Siemen's. He never went to sea again. Others tried to change tack, like Bertie Fry:

> I swallowed the anchor then, for we couldn't lay at Gravesend doing nothing with nothing coming in. I worked in the cement works, but I couldn't take it. Then I went pulverising coal, but I was closed in; I simply couldn't take four walls round me. I'd come home like a sweep, coughing it up. I had to give it up. It was the same all round – Mr. Naylor down the road, he was a hand sail-maker; there were no more barges being made, and he threw in the sponge too. I was unemployed for a bit, then I joined the cement packing plant, then, you'll never believe this, I was an engine driver, I never had to steer that thing! I was driving my engine, pulling trucks of rail staves behind me, but I went back. I couldn't breathe in all that. Anyway I got back as a Freeman; my grandfather, his grandfather, Nanny's dad, a London waterman, my brother-in-law, we were all Freemen and I couldn't change. But I had to eat crow, though – I went back on a Dutch motor barge.

Many others, like Charlie Jackson, left London temporarily to apply their skill to areas where a sailorman's know-how was needed. He packed his bags after applying to the life-boat service, and started with a somewhat mature apprenticeship as a prospective mechanic in Galston with Joe Johnson and the *John & Mary Macklin*. He didn't exactly have engine oil running through his veins, but a house went with the job.

Thames Sailing Barge skipper and wife mate, 1900's, with eeling spear.

❦13❧

High Days and Holidays

Let's have a basinful of the briny
Where the breeze blow, blow, blow, blows.
Let's have a basinful of the briny,
Where the shrimps and winkles grow.
Oh it's grand to watch the breakers
Rolling in for holiday-makers.
Oh, let's have a basinful of the briny
Where the breezes blow, blow, blow.

Music hall song

UPRIVER THERE WERE still the traditional high days and holidays when nagging worries could be put aside. The highspot of the Freeman's year was still Doggett's Coat and Badge race. Then there was the Oxford and Cambridge boat race when Nellie Shackel with other Battersea lightermen's children, were poled up screaming their heads off on their respective dads' lighters, to the envy, I suspect, of more well-endowed children ashore who had to be hoisted up on shoulders. Each area had its own regatta, and that at Bankside was organised each year in the 20s and 30s by lighterman Bobbie Bush, and sweating contestants would be accompanied by a resplendent brass band clinging perilously to an old tram on a lighter pulled by a steam tug, until the heroic strains of 'See the Conquering Hero Come' were lost in spumes of black smoke and stifled choking.

The annual Whitebait Festival at the Trafalgar Pub when festive barges had plied between Swan Stairs and Greenwich Pier, sadly ended in 1857, for the catch could no longer go straight from a net at the water's edge into the pot. But ashore there was still the Greenwich Fair when thousands of Cockneys escaped to one of the lungs of London. It was held on Easter Monday and ran for three wild days of ginger-beer, stout and fresh shrimps, con-men with their surreptitious suit-cases opening and shutting, "Pick a card – it's as easy as falling off a log", and enterprising pensioners at Greenwich Hospital who would guide gullible tourists to the site of the hulks for a tanner. The fair was attended by dozens of up-country gypsies and a good half dozen assorted brass bands. Lost to time are the tented melodrama theatres and the huge marquee dancing arena at The Rose & Crown, charging a bob at the door.

Up until 1872 (although it was unofficially celebrated in the 1920s), crowds would have made their riotous way up to Charlton House each St. Luke's Day for the Annual Horn Fair where an obscure notice would be read to them. Then the procession would march off again to Cuckold's Point in Deptford in celebration of an occasion definitely vulgar, and I suppose it is the more prudish parishioners we have to thank for its virtual disappearance. For at Cuckold's Point the crowd would turn ceremoniously and march back to Charlton House with assorted phallic symbols including a decorated maypole. All this was said to be in celebration of bad King John who had tumbled a miller's daughter and been caught with his trousers down by an irate father who was not impressed by the divine right of Kings. The legend has it that John offered him all the land he could encompass in one glance, and the miller fell for it, discovering later that he could see no further than a large hill on Limehouse Point – it's known as Cuckold's Point to this day. The tradition went that he had to re-establish his boundaries once a year by erecting a pole and a pair of horns on what is now Charlton Park, so 'Horn Fair' it was. It still pops up to this day in the occasional school fete.

The early years of the 1930s were potmarked with uncertainty, but those lucky few who were insured under the new Government scheme could obtain a little money to make ends meet, although people still speak of the humiliation of the 'means test' man walking down the road, and it's certain that for the 23 per cent registered unemployed in 1932, there was a great submerged number who were too proud to claim their rights. Immigration increased into London from the North East and Scotland where the unemployment figures were a horrendous 28 per cent, and that's counting only the insured. For sure it was a comfortable time for the professional family. New garden suburbs were sprouting satellites from a dozen corners of London's sprawl, and places like Eltham, till then a tiny rustic village, disappeared under tarmac and semis when the mortgage rate was 4½ per cent, and the buying price around £450, which was the average annual wage for a schoolmaster. For the riverside, however, a 50 m.p.g. Austin 7 for £125 was a bit steep, and a good percentage of the 724,000 motor-bikes and sidecars which adorned England's roads came from dockland and riverside. However, a packet of six Ogden's 'Robin' cigarettes cost twopence, and if the weather was good, the average family tended to get away for a 'beano' – that word which has crept into our language from the annual Woolwich Arsenal 'beanfeast' instituted by King George III one sunny July day in 1773. Even if some chose to spend their picnic day uptown listening to Oswald Mosley and his new British Fascist Party screaming the advantages of a one party state and the necessity for stripping all Jews of their British nationality, most made the best of a good day by escaping the smoke. Charlie Jackson recalls:

> When I was a youngster, I went to the Band of Hope each Sunday, and you paid your penny for a day out in the country on Sakers' horse-drawn brakes with two, sometimes four horses, and often a brass-band playing along with us. We'd go to the Bull of Birchwood in Swanley, Kent, or to Theydon Bois. It was marvellous. Some of the people went hopping for the summer to earn a bit and have a holiday at the same time but that was more your Cockney's holiday, really. Before the garden suburbs were built at Eltham and Welling, folks might go hopping there, coming back home in the evening. The scoopers used to leave with carts carrying everything; mattresses, cooking pots, jerries, all piled up. Then if we had just a bit of time to ourselves, we'd spend the day on Greenwich beach; just like the seaside that was, well, crowds of city folk thought that *was* the seaside. If the weather was bad, it was penny lantern slides at the Assembly Rooms, Woolwich, or the threepenny bughutch with the old girl on the piano, or the farthing's worth of locust beans up the back of Barnard's Music Hall. 'Course, that was earlier. By 1930 that had gone, and all the girls were grizzling in the stalls over *The Jazz Singer*.

For the great mass of people the typical Londoner's holiday was a day out at Southend, and for Bob Sargent a free day out because his uncle worked on the *Golden Eagle*. There must be a million Londoners at least who recall the excitement of crowding on her as she thumped down to Southend where deckchairs were opened on the narrow strip of shingle above the mud, handkerchiefs knotted in four corners, and trousers rolled up for a paddle and a look at the wild marshes of the Kentish side. Nellie Shackel was one:

> In the early days, we saved ten shillings up for a fortnight's holiday – ten shillings for Country Holiday Fun it was called. The farms took one or two kids each. Then there were day trips to Southend which was full of shellfish stalls and arcades. The whole street would go in one party. That's why so many Londoners still have chalets on Canvey Island – that was as far as you could afford to go then, so roots were dropped there.

The sailorman, however, was luckier – if he got a good freight, he would combine work and pleasure and take his family with him, and Bertie Fry, working a Dutch M.V. by this time, could give his family the only holidays they could snatch. Nanny Fry remembers:

> If we had something to do around the islands, then we'd all go, taking the boys and Grandad on the Dutch barge; she was a beauty, all brass rails, even a sitting room. I kept my potted plants there. The cabins were lovely, all wood. No ladder in her, but stairs, and even a small state room with brass hanging lamps. The water was like glass in those creeks, and I seemed to spend all my time making bread and jam for the boys. I used to be washing up all the time, throwing a pail over the side to draw up water. I don't think one wash-up went by when I hadn't thrown a cup or fork overside. That's the lot, I'd think, and then look over the side and see half a dozen knives lying on the bottom. The boys would go off fishing, and I'd fish for cutlery; funny I should remember that particularly . . .

For my family, memories of 'mudding' down at Allhallows initiated an annual pilgrimage, which by my time had progressed to good canvas tents and shiny outboard engines, but in the 30s slump, it was partly a holiday, and partly a cheaper way of getting over the slim weeks. Uncle Con explained:

> Apart from the slump itself, we went for the air. London was thick with coal-soot and fog then. The Essex side of the river would be crowded with people, thousands of them, and we could see ferries

weaving backwards and forwards to the pier, but that was not our way; we went to the Kentish side, to the marshes. There was hardly a soul there, except a London woman and her son. He had tuberculosis and she kept hoping the air would do him good. Later they practically moved there permanently, that old girl and her son coughing his heart up. We had sewn our own tent from old sails and odd bits of tarpaulin, and had one or two oil-lamps. Duck shooting or rabbit snaring then wasn't for fun, it was because the pennies were a bit short. Each day we'd send the girls over the planks to the village for bread, and to the butchers, but nine times out of ten he'd say, "Come back in an hour, I haven't killed it yet." There was a lot going on round that coast, black as ink at night and not a soul round the sea-wall. On one occasion somebody or other tried to 'haunt' us off the marshes. We never did discover what the white shapes floating over the dykes at night were. With money short, anything could have been going on, immigrants from Europe or smuggling. I remember one night in the late thirties, we woke up to hear lions roaring, definitely lions; we thought we'd all gone barmy, but years later that mystery was solved for it was around the time of the phony war, and animals from the upriver zoos had been moved to Slough Fort which was disused at the time.

Whitsun camping on the marshes at Allhallows, smoking fish and hunting for crabs.

The estuary community's big day was the Annual Sailing Barge Race when upriver and coastal bargemen would vie for the coveted cup. A dozen little houses today still give pride of place to their inscribed medals – Bertie Fry had two, and Skipper Percy Mitchell of Bromley in Kent wrote to tell me of his family who had held the Championship of the River Thames and Medway for several years from 1898 with S.B. *Giralda*. The races were usually held from June, out of Southend, Chatham, Greenwich itself, Erith to the Nore and back in Kent, and from Pin Mill, the Swale and Blackwater on the Eastern side. It had all started in 1863 as the brainchild of an ex-ploughboy called Henry Dodd who had made a packet from rubbish disposal upriver, and was known as 'The Golden Dustman'. His intentions hadn't been entirely aesthetic because the annual race led to improvements in design and speed of the barges, but it did improve the status of the skippers concerned. When he died in 1881 he left a sum of money for the relief of poor bargemen, and his elaborate burial vault depicting a team of plough horses and a fleet of barges displayed his own choice of epitaph. 'Originator of the Sailing Barge Races. True School of the Navy.' Many of the cement fleets numbered some fine racing craft amongst their old packhorses, such as *Grebe, Whaup, Coot, Iota* and *Northumberland*. Originally, a winner one year was not allowed to compete the next. No ballast was carried, and up to five hands were allowed, if they were fully employed during the race, and of course, extra sail was carried. However, by 1931 the cement companies were scrapping their fleets or stripping them down to install engines, and the huge start-lines which had once crowded sail with inches to spare between them, were sadly diminished, but the Barge Race survives.

Back home at Riverside, in a succession of bright summers broken by sudden storms, there was, as everywhere else, a feeling of impending change. The Arsenal bell had ceased to ring, and the one o'clock gun no longer fired. Perhaps people who live near an Arsenal pick up waves sooner than others, perhaps it is an inherent instinct in people who could be blown to kingdom come any minute, but the prevailing feeling during the 30s was a determination to make hay while the sun shone. At the docks the free trade which London had enjoyed for centuries came to an end in 1932. Strange crazes like 'Cheerio Yo, Yo' juxtaposed with police baton charges in Hyde Park. In 1931 *Graf Zeppelin* buzzed nosily over London with cameras clicking every facet of dock layout, and delegations of visiting

Japanese and German technicians paused with uncommon interest over Seimen's work-benches. Lightermen passing the Tower of London in 1932 looked up and argued over which cell held Lt. Norman Baillie-Stewart who had sold secrets to the Germans and was the first prisoner in the Tower for generations, and they quipped that if he'd given them the secrets he'd have been promoted to captain. These were the years when two and two definitely made five. At home people sang:

> As a listener to wireless I'm absolutely tireless,
> I'm devoted to my little crystal set,
> All the music's so seductive,
> Tho' I 'ate the more instructive
> Of the items in the programmes wot we get . . .

and Charlton riversiders were more disgruntled by Arsenal winning the 1933 F.A. Cup than the fact that Herr Hitler was now Chancellor of Germany.

The old Woolwich ferries had been replaced by *Will Crooks* and *John Benn* and most of Forty Corners had been demolished to make way for a spanking new pier. With 8,000 unemployed in Woolwich alone, however, some of the old missions there had been hastily propped up again as makeshift workrooms where unemployed could earn a few bob mending boots, and for a time pig-breeding returned to the allotments where Saxon hogs had grubbed a thousand years before. Local church sermons were beginning to exhort riverside parishioners to 'extend the hand of friendship' to unspecified foreign powers, although nobody listening needed three guesses, for hundreds of Jewish refugees were daily arriving from Antwerp at the George V Docks seeking asylum. George V died and the following year of unsettling wrangles ended with the unprecedented abdication of Edward VIII.

More and more cargoes were coming in swaddled by security, and A. Steatham, who had been brought up in Greenwich and longed for the day when he could take sail, found himself as an apprentice in 1937 on the steam-tug *Enid Blanche*.

Everything on the docks was mad busy; nobody knew why there was such a rush, but we were raising steam at six a.m. of a Monday morning, and her fires weren't allowed to die until late Saturday night. Old *Enid*

Blanche was back and forth twenty-four hours a day with three crews working twelve hours on twelve hours off. I was a tug-boy earning thirty-two shillings a week and in between trying to get my Freeman's papers studying the sets of the tide and sweeping on the steel lighters.

Captain Dick Virgo noted heavier traffic than ever in the Pool, and strange chemicals which were covering the water from Silvertown. "In the 20s, the River Police had used the South West India Docks for life-saving classes, but as time went by we were noticing the Thames did funny things to your paintwork. Blue turned black, and white turned pink. I remember one day in the Albert, the water stunk so bad they poured some solution into it; it was like wallowing in a large jug of milk."

In July of that year the borough held a 'Peace Week', and there were showings of films like *War is Hell*, which everybody agreed was true, but unfortunately nobody had told the Germans, and the Arsenal went on recruiting more and more men and women. In 1938 the area buzzed with rumours concerning the secret trial of four Arsenal workers and the mysterious Miss X. who'd collared them at sabotage.

People earning less than five pounds a week were being exhorted to collect their Anderson Shelters. In 1939 dockland held its first 'mock air-raid'. All lights were extinguished, kerbs painted white, and police on their new B.S.A. motor-bikes roared round Riverside rattles clattering over their heads.

In the two uneasy years before war broke out, everybody at least knew the score: watermen were utilised as coastal watches, and stripped barges were moored along the estuary as barrage balloon stations. Hitler's war directives of 1939 stipulated, "Attacks on the principal English ports by mining and blocking the sea-lanes leading to them", and "aircraft are extremely valuable in mine-laying – particularly outside English West Coast ports, in narrow waterways, and in river estuaries . . ."

Nelson's early *river Fencibles*, took to the water again, and others joined the Land Defence Volunteers, soon nicknamed the 'Look, Duck and Vanish Brigade', now better remembered as the Home Guard. Some riversiders, like Uncle Con, found themselves in situations bordering on burlesque.

I was intended for the Navy, but at first was kept on at Siemen's for reserved work. Then came a spell of defence before I joined up proper. I was sent to the Fleet Air Arm at Lee-on-Solent. There were truck-loads of rusty old guns, from museums some of them; none of them worked, it was just to make the coastal guard look good from the air. One corner of the marsh was decked out to look like a machine-gun nest. The weapon was there all right, but it had no barrel, so we stuck a piece of plumber's lead pipe in it, and pointed it up at the sky. Days went by, and I still didn't have a gun. Eventually I was issued with a pike from the Tower of London. When I'd been working at Siemen's, we'd been experimenting with a cathode-ray tube which had picked out dots on the coast: suddenly the channel seemed very narrow. I'd bought a pair of plimsolls on a trip home, and kept them in a bag by my side. There was a small copse near our post, and frankly, if I'd seen the Jerries coming up that beach I think I would have run like hell. Most fellers had carved wooden guns. I mean, what could we have done? Splinter them to death? It was the biggest bluff of all time. Why, there was a hillock near us with some Home Guard stationed on it and all they had were drums full of petrol. If they saw the enemy approaching they were supposed to ignite the drums and roll them down the hill.

Bob Sargent recalled the muddle during the 'Phony War':

> The Navy had zoned the river; different pilots responsible for different zones. They didn't know what to do with us skilled men; kept calling us up into the Navy then sending us back – backwards and forwards. A lot of the lightermen went into an outfit designed to help with the landings. We called it Harry Tate's Navy. Two brothers went into that. Leslie was shipwrecked in the landings and Ronnie and I were piloting vessels upriver. We were badly overstretched; the world and his brother seemed to be coming up that Reach. I remember the first time Ronnie went solo; he wasn't strictly qualified, but he piloted a Norwegian ship loaded to the gills with explosives. He must have lost a stone.

For many of the close-knit community in Riverside, it was the end of an era in more ways than one. Uncle Con describes how the demolition men moved in in 1938: "When they demolished West Street, we all piled on a cart with the old lady on the back holding the goldfish bowl. Virtually all they had to do was go to the end of the street and push – those houses came down like a pack of cards . . ." There were sixteen left standing.

On September 1st, 1939 a great crocodile of giggling children, with labels in their collars and Mickey Mouse gas-masks over their shoulders, lined up behind the school caretaker to board the pleasure

steamers which were to take them on a last big beano to the East
Anglian and Kentish farmsteads where it was thought German
bombers could not reach. That night older men acting as 'Jim
Crows' climbed up on riverside rooftops to wait for the enemy
whom everybody by now knew would follow the reconnaissance
aircraft which had been coming for weeks despite Mr. Chamberlain's
bit of paper. With the paradoxical sensation which people recall as
something like relief, riverside Londoners heard war declared on
September 3rd, 1939. At least they knew where they were – right in
the middle of Hitler's 'narrow waterways and river estuaries . . .'

❧ 14 ❧

Some Particularly Favourable Target

'A Lake in Hell . . .'

A. P. Herbert

THE EVENTS OF THE Second World War spread a stain over every corner of Britain. Nobody escaped without bruises of one kind or another: the loss of a friend, relation, husband, son or daughter, and it is all too easy to take an overall view in the safe distance of the 70s, rather like Cecil B. De Mille editing an all-time blockbusting epic where a million extras are seen like ants, and not a single close-up occurs to personalise and focus the thousands of small, everyday incidents into breathing reality. How can we know the spirit of people living right in the middle of Hitler's dockland target? Or the feelings of sailing barge skippers on coastal runs as they look up to see a Messerschmitt dropping down on them: "where some particularly favourable target happens to present itself . . . for the training of our air crews". (Directive August 17th, 1940, sub-paragraph 3.)

The war was made up of thousands of sub-paragraphs, within them small people trying to make do; events beyond their grasp, reasons not clear until it was all over. Two wars killed 36,000 merchant seamen alone, but produced a generation of children healthier than ever before, despite ration diets where a family might see no more than thirty-one eggs in a year, and ordinary people

Grain Fort was manned until 1956; these photographs were taken in 1958. It was demolished in 1962 to make way for the Isle of Grain power station.

sampled the delights of whale and horsemeat fashioned into Mr. Oxley's meat bricks (more could be stowed in a ship's holds when in cubes). It was an age of Morrison shelters, where children slept in small cages under tables and often woke up to find their homes round their ears, and neighbours crowding into one surviving wreck where the gas stove was functioning and tea could still be brewed. For me it is a dim memory of an old lady in a black beret standing on a heap of roof-tiles, a ripped oil-painting clasped to her breast. Who she was I don't know – not even whether she was there at all – but the memory persists. It was these kind of memories that floated to the minds of people I talked to, and leaving aside the 'whys' and 'wherefores' of the grand pattern, if there ever was one. It was these I wanted to record.

Many of the traditional sailing barge skippers were beyond active service age by 1940, and of course the majority of the younger men were hived off into the services, particularly the Royal and Merchant Navies. The parochial communities of dockers, lightermen and bargemen never returned to the same insularity after the war. In many cases they had no homes to return to, or had developed a taste for other areas during spells of evacuation. Many settled in the ports where they had been transferred for war work, such as the large party of London dockers and lightermen who departed for the Clyde and its emergency port, or upriver families seconded to tiny coastal harbours grown big by war. In fact there wasn't an overseas action which involved a strip of shallow water with goods to be landed which did not have its contingent of Thames lightermen, dockers and tugmen in uniform, even as far afield as Burma.

LBV Mk 1 No 44.

The Axis were spot on with their magnetic mines dropped in both estuary and upalong, and dozens of old barges found a temporary lease of life with their immune wooden hulls. Both barges and lighters emerged from refitting docks bristling with weird accoutrements under the control of the R.A.S.C.'s Water Transport Section, and old Thames sailing barges hitherto accustomed to the tread of only one skipper and one mate found themselves once more crammed with officers and ratings, top heavy ramps, machine-guns and tanks for fresh water and no less than two cuddies – one for officers, one for O/Rs.

In an age when technological warfare reached a pinnacle, sailor-men using the technique of Francis Drake carried on trading, like the *Will Everard* which completed 147 coastal trips along shorelines where enemy fire could be clearly seen over the Channel, and where an adverse calm or broken tow rope could drift the unarmed skipper and his mate into the range of enemy guns.

Charlie Jackson was still in the life-boat service at Dover, and Bertie Fry was coasting coal for the Margate Gas Company. It was Dick Virgo of the London & Rochester Company who experienced the sudden security net which descended in May 1940 to herald Dunkirk. "I went to the Lobster pub to ring for my orders, and was told 'You can't use the phone.' I could see dozens of barges being towed downriver, all under the Navy which was a bit strange. 'They won't let you get through,' I was told, 'it's all secret.'"

Skipper Godwin recalls the urgency:

Well, I had this load of sand for Ford's, and along comes a Naval vessel. "In there!" he shouted through his megaphone. He wanted me to turn into Tilbury Basin. "I'm not going in there, I've got sand for Fords!" I shouted back. "Get int!" he shouted, and hit me on the bow, wouldn't even give me a chance to take down my sails. We got into Tilbury Basin, all my paintwork scratched to blazes, and there must have been eighty barges crammed in there. They wouldn't brook no argument at all. We were kept waiting for a long time, me and my missus. None of us could turn in. Eventually they came round over the barges, and gave us each four pounds and some corn beef rations and bread. We knew there was a push on, of course; well, folks down at Dover and Deal could see the gunfire for themselves. Anyway, four of the biggest barges were marked, and at about four a.m. they said to us, "It's all off, you can go!" So we did. But it was chaos getting that number of barges out. The four biggest, 180 tonners or thereabouts, stayed for whatever-it-was. Well, we all would have gone if asked, but believe you me, there was no volunteering, at that stage we had no option.

On Riverside, tool-makers looked up from their lathes and out on to the water to see hundreds of small craft of every size, shape and description, including paddle steamers chugging downriver past Siemen's, and some joker said it was probably the invasion fleet. Bob Sargent answered the call for boats with his little *Jeannette*, "but in the event, I didn't have to go". He returned to the Anchor and Hope where his mother was still holding the fort.

However, *Pudge*, belonging to the London & Rochester Trading

Company, was one which took part in the evacuation. She had been loading at Tilbury for Ipswich, and she and her gold-earringed skipper, Bill Watson, were ordered to Dover, where a Naval officer asked for volunteers to evacuate troops from Dunkirk, on what was officially called 'Operation Dynamo'. All ten skippers assembled volunteered, and *Pudge* together with *Thyra* and *Lady Roseberry* (both pure sail) were towed out by *St. Fabian*, an Admiralty tug, which had not been 'degaussed' against magnetic mines. Just off Dunkirk *Pudge* started her auxiliary motor and had just pulled away when the tug hit a mine. *Thyra*, *Lady Roseberry*, and *St. Fabian* completely disappeared, and Bill stopped to pick up survivors, including the stoker of the tug who had miraculously escaped. The skipper and mate were just debating whether to 'bugger off back to Dover' when a destroyer came alongside and ordered them into Ramsgate. In all, sixteen barges took part in the evacuation of Dunkirk between May 27th and June 4th, and eight were lost. *Ethel Everard* sister-barge to *Will Everard* being strafed on coastal runs, was, like *Royalty*, blown up when she was full to the brim with ammunition, and *Aidie*, *Barbara Jean*, *Doris*, and *Duchess* were also destroyed. *Beatrice Maud* had been abandoned in a fog, and was boarded by 250 soldiers who managed to get her moving. She was rescued from a sandbank by a trawler and towed back home. The similarly abandoned *Ena* performed an even more remarkable feat. Obviously not caring for the flak, she sailed herself back home to Sandwich unattended.

There were other evacuations in June from St. Valéry-en-Caux, Le Havre, Cherbourg, and Brest, when *Cabby* the last full-size wooden sail-barge built in 1928 and named after a favourite bulldog of the L. & R.'s director was requisitioned on her way to Scotland. Her skipper, Captain Harry Rands, landed a full load of soldiers safely at Plymouth, before she continued up north where she spent the war. Fifteen thousand troops arrived in Woolwich to be billeted. "I saw some of the Dunkirk soldiers in and around the pubs in Woolwich. I've never seen men looking more white and frozen. Most were joking, glad to be alive, but there were some there who were still in shock."

The Armada of little vessels which helped to lift half a million men off the beaches, where sprit-sailed vessels were strategically used in battle for the first time since the Orange Wars, conceals stories of incredible risk, and yet it is very difficult to winkle details from people who were involved, Bertie Fry, for example, was more explicit about his run-ins with the British Navy than the German, which was regularly strafing vessels on coastal runs. Nanny Fry showed me a cryptic telegram: SAFE STOP BE HOME TONIGHT STOP

I was coasting. I lost a ship. It was very dark, and we managed to grab a compass and get a sail up. The Cromer life-boat – Coxswain Briggs his name was, God rest him – picked us up, and I sent that telegram to Mum. Much later I was carrying high octane fuel for the Omaha beach landings. No more of that, thanks! What I remember most was the Navy; sometimes they acted like we were on the other side, you know. I don't expect fishing trawler skippers will mind me mentioning it either. We didn't ask for any medals, nothing of that sort, but we weren't respected by the Navy; why, most of the skippers were made petty officers at the most, not even commissioned.

I can remember one time, I was being examined by this lieutenant when I was skipper of a 600 tonner. He was asking me if I'd seen anything suspicious, and I'm thinking as the ratings are stamping around, I know you from somewhere. His manner didn't invite conversation, but I kept thinking to myself, I've seen him before . . . Curiosity got the better of me, and I said, "Don't I know you, sir?" (I'm the ship's master and I'm calling him 'sir'). "I don't think so," he says, looking me up and down. Then I get it. "Aren't you the landlord of the Dog and Duck?" Was his face red! I'd been in his pub playing darts before the war, and now he thinks he's everybody.

The Navy and the sailorman were all doing the same job, but you wouldn't have thought so. All we asked was our 'due', but the nearest I ever got to it was one time off Plymouth. I'm not boasting, but there isn't a port I don't know, but when the war came, we had to have a pilot. Every time a Naval bloke would climb aboard and waste time. I didn't need a bloody pilot, and one time, the nearest I got to some respect, was this lieutenant. He sat back and folded his arms and said, "Carry on. You know more about this coast than I do, let me learn from you." Oh, he was picking my brains, but it was worth it. I thought the Navy would bend a bit after the First War, but no, all the old rank business came out again. Thousands of merchant boys went down: they deserve their due.

On September 7th, the war came to dockland with a vengeance. Around five p.m. on a gloriously sunny day, 'Jim Crows' spotted 375 bombers heading upriver for the heart of the docks. Everybody there has a story to tell, and putting together the jigsaw of isolated on-the-spot witnesses, the dreadful statistics take a personal, and sometimes grimly humorous tone. Astonishingly, people carried on with the same bloody-mindedness that has typified the riverside through centuries. The sky blackened with bombers, and for one hour and forty minutes the area of Beckton, Charlton, East and West Ham, and the docks were engulfed in an inferno. Charlie Jackson takes up the story:

> I'd given up the life-boats, got fed up with being moved around all over the place. I'd worked for a bit on *Magog* the big lighter at Shoeburyness, then gone back to Woolwich Arsenal. There was a call for blokes who were willing to drive lorries up to Liverpool. You never knew what was in them, you just had a card marked with four stars, and red flags to warn people off. I decided that the missus needed a holiday, and we set off together, right in the middle of the air-raid. The docks below us were a ring of fire. I drove off like a bat out of hell. Some holiday for the missus. I didn't know what we were carrying, but from the reaction we got from the Army, we knew it wasn't cotton wool. One time in Liverpool all the dockers unhitched the crates, took one look, and scattered in all directions.

Tom Sadler was sunning himself on a lighter at Millwall Roads. "Suddenly there was a droning, and then the water was on fire, ropes caught, barges started to explode, and you could see that all the timber in the Surrey and Commercial had caught. Parts of the river was floating flames."

In the Royal Docks the blazing air was sweetened by the sickly smell of burning rum, and black smoke choked the wharves along the rubber warehouses. Ignited sugar spilt down Gallions. People on the Isle of Dogs were cut off by a wall of fire, and Bob Sargent pushed *Jeannette* from its moorings:

> Greenwich Tunnel was flooded, and our faces were getting scorched – we had to wrap ourselves in wet towels. I was rowing backwards and forwards with *Jeannette*. There was a stream of women and children, all standing up to their arm-pits in water, many of them with their babies over their heads. We just snatched them up and dumped them in the boats then rowed back, dodging falling embers. Funny thing, just a couple of years ago I got a letter from a woman living in Australia – she was one of the kiddies I'd ferried out that night.

The bombers could not have come at a worse time nor had such good weather conditions, for the sunshine had brought out hundreds of people, and the docks were working at full swing.

Several barges simply disappeared in the debris. *Enchantress* was crushed as the Rank Flour Mill toppled on to her in the Albert Docks. By six forty, the 'all clear' was sounded, and people began to pick out the fifty-three dead and 247 injured in the Arsenal. East and West Ham alone had 33,000 buildings damaged, and 85 per cent of one square acre in the tidal basin was completely flattened. Before anyone had time to collect accurate figures, the bombers were back, using the fires as beacons. It was to go on all night, and yet, astonishingly, there was still the obstinate stoic who refused to call it a day. Mr. Steatham recalled:

> Five other lightermen and myself had just completed a tour from Hammersmith to Limehouse, and by the time we had finished mooring the barges to the roads, it was about one o'clock in the morning. The Blitz was at its height with parachute flares slowly descending and turning night into day, and oil bombs burning riverside warehouses, with 'H.E.' bombs raining to stoke them up. It was hell. So the tug skipper said, "Well lads, the roadsman's ashore in his dug-out. Where do ye want me to put your ashore?" so I said, "Greenwich Pier, Joe."
>
> So we headed downriver, and sure enough he put me out as requested. By this time, around two a.m., things were really warming up and as I walked up to the Promenade, the pierman came out of his hut and said, "Where's yer penny, mate?" (The landing fee on L.C.C. piers was a penny) I was so astounded I paid him!

The 'all clear' did not sound until four thirty the following morning, and it went on for another fifty-seven nights, all night every night until November 2nd. Despite the subsequent years of 'doodlebugs', V.1s and V.2s nothing really surpassed that first night. The reverberations stretched right down to the estuary and Medway, as Dick Virgo carrying torpedo heads for two and a half years at Upnor remembered:

> That day in September, we could see the smoke from upriver. As they passed back this way, they dropped what they had left over Kent. Otterham Creek was bombed, and they killed one cow and one soldier. Most of them landed in the mud and didn't go off. Gawd knows how many are still out there; coastal fishermen are constantly trawling them up. Two of my mates had gone victualling up at the Scapa Flow with *Alderman* and *Knowles*. There were set afire and sunk there.

This was the time when people really believed in their number coming up, and certainly, some seemed to be charmed one way or another. Mr. Steatham recalls two occasions in the Blitz:

After November, the Luftwaffe resorted to 'nuisance raids': on a low-cloud day for example, the air-raid siren would be on and off all day, and a few Heinkels would prowl about dropping bombs here and there. At one time I was being towed upriver, and was just abreast of Bay Wharf behind which are two huge gas-holders of the East Greenwich gas works. Suddenly this bomber dived through a hole in the clouds right overhead. Another cloud must have obscured the gasometers because he didn't drop anything. Another time I thought my number was up was as I worked up Greenwich Reach. I was abreast of Greenwich Naval College, and we knew the river had been mined. Just ahead of me, a tug and barges disappeared in a terrific bang and column of water – there were deaths with that one.

The luck of the draw proved its point time and time again. Charlie Jackson delivered his lorry load to Liverpool, with his wife and himself alone unloading it, and Bob Sargent just happened to be away from the Old Ship Hotel in Greenwich where he was then lodging, when it received a direct hit in the last of the saturation blitzes that November. For others, like Nellie Shackel, the dice played cruelly:

Each night we'd sleep in the shelter, and that bad night we took a bit of a bashing, three people were killed just a few doors up. We were all right though, Mum, Dad, me and the three kids and my cousin. Dad was working still in the docks with the Sullivans up the road; they were lightermen too. The Peace Party was good, but it rained, and my cousin who'd shared the shelter with us all that time died of T.B. on D-Day – to go through all that and then die at the end, it didn't seem fair.

With 600 barges in commission as storage hulks, mine-patrols and barrage-balloon stations, not to mention those in Holy Loch and on the beaches at Normandy, older skippers found themselves in some strange places during the war, and Charlie Jackson's progress through the five years to 1945 shows some of the odd guises in which sailormen found themselves:

I thought I was using up my nine lives rather fast with the lorries, and I wanted the feel of water again, so I got myself posted to Vernon Dockyard running despatches in a beautiful speedboat which had belonged to General Ironsides who was in Malta. It was a real monster, three Napier engines in her. Nobby Clark from Woolwich was my engineer. She was all fitted out with green leather inside; it was a bit posher than my old cuddy and did twenty-six knots. I was told to go and get some orders at the office. I was there all day. When I came back they'd stripped her of all the plush, painted her battleship grey and called her *Quail*. I spent ten minutes walking up and down looking for her; didn't recognise her at all. Then we were sent to Ryde on the Isle of Wight to test searchlights, backwards and forwards on fixed headings all night. God, it was boring; couldn't show a light, make a cup of tea, nothing. Just backwards and forwards with the vibration shaking your teeth loose, and black as the ace of spades. Couple of nights like this and me and Nobby are getting browned off. Anyway, one night Nobby has an idea. The *Courageous* is lying out there, a naval aircraft carrier. Why don't we go behind her, tie off, make a cup of tea and play a hand of cards while they play with their searchlights? So we did. Next night: "Same time tonight, sir?" "Same time tonight, skipper." That night behind the *Courageous* cuppa tea, cards. At the end of the week the officer congratulates us for evading his searchlights. "I done the best I could, sir," I says.

We shouldn't have been so smart because they'd twigged us from the beginning. I was sent to Christchurch for an 'experiment'. We'd go out with an Army officer with a load of little red and white balls, and he'd give me a precise heading or locality and then these little balls would be dropped overside. A minute later there'd be a great whoosh and a bang with water chutes going up just a few yards away, and there's this officer grinning all over his face. "What's the matter with you, skipper? It's only a little bang." We were laying targets for long-range precision gunnery. I had weeks of those shells whizzing past. Teach me to try and do the Navy.

Twelve dockers had been stowing a Sicily invasion vessel in 1943 when it received orders to sail immediately with them on board. The London docks must have appeared a strange sight when they managed to get themselves home over a year later. Upstream docks were full of refitting Naval warships, and huge cruisers stood in the Royals. In the Surrey Docks enormous fortresses towered on stilts ready to be towed out to the estuary like so many gigantic trees. The East India had been pumped dry to build massive Mulberry harbours, and on D-Day itself, 194 ships loaded along with 1,000 barges to join the 209 other D-Day ships of which Bertie Fry's small petrol coaster was one. Riversiders watched the biggest armada the Thames had ever known passing on its way to Normandy.

Hopeful sailormen returned to their Thames sailing barges to find, in many cases, that years of inactivity as storage hulks had opened them to the worm, and relations with the Navy still hadn't improved one jot:

In 1945 [said Dick Virgo] I did six minesweeps with my old *Acorn*. A worm had got right through her. We filled up fast and had to pump all the time; the old girl was in a rum shape. We'd pumped her by nine o'clock, and the Navy comes up. I told them we were taking water and that's why were so slow, but they wouldn't believe us. I'd made several bungs with old rags, and we were dry for a bit, so this Navy bloke don't believe me.

"You're not making water," he says. "You sail barges are just old and slow, that's what it is!"

So I pulls the bung out. "Oh, ain't I?" I says. "There y'are, boyo. I'll bloody soon make her do it agen."

Three quarters of our fleet was finished by drying out, weeds or the worm from standing still too long.

The masters and mates never came to terms with the Navy.

The London & Rochester Company's sailing barges were also badly depleted by the war's end. The Government compensated their loss handsomely, and companies like London & Rochester used the money to buy motor barges. It was the end of an era.

✤ 15 ✤

The Turning Tide

> Has some vast imbecility
> Mighty to build and blend,
> But impotent to tend,
> Framed us in jest, and left us now to hazardry?
>
> Thomas Hardy

IN THE FADING years of the 40s the docks were still busy, with a count of some 6,000 barges and lighters, and 136 colliers plying between London and the North to supply fourteen electricity stations and three gasworks up tributaries and canals. Times were changing, however, things moving on. The world of the people who worked the river, using ancient skills and techniques is dying with them, while the river itself is becoming lost to sight behind tower blocks of offices, and wire-fences with no heed to ancient rights of way, and before too long, nobody will be around to uphold those rights. Riverfront pubs which people like Mr. Steatham recall as sawdust-floored refresher rooms for armies of lightermen and dockies, have become places to go on chic Sunday outings for up-towners, and the old crumbling waterfront cottages near the Angel tavern are now the desirable property of tycoons and personalities. When people do try to revitalise the riverfront by installing small craftsmen at Rotherhithe, the G.L.C. gives them their inch, and then slaps prohibitive rate demands on already slender means; 'answerable to nones' erect ugly blockhouses to cram in tourists at St. Katharines, and one wonders how long the three barges moored there will survive the profit incentive before they get their marching orders to make way for lucrative millionaires' yachts.

Warehouses, once busy with the noise of carts and toil, rot into the mud, whilst speculators wait for the market to boom, and the stray old riversider squats outside with his pint because his local disdains his appearance and he feels out of place in his own place. Downriver on the estuary, the dykes and ditches which were once tended to hive off the worst of a high spring tide, are left to silt up, and a new yacht club at Allhallows encloses its fibre-glass charges in a fine new fence, proclaiming as Private Property that free stretch of shoreline fashioned by sandies. At Riverside the Thames barrage with a planned bulk of ten gates, each the size of a five storey building, presses on to a 1980 completion, with a new sense of urgency since the winter of 1977 when the river rose a few inches too many and gave rise to hundreds of warning posters in Underground stations, and a moment's sensation in the media. The once busy Surrey and Commercial Dock has, ironically, returned in small part to its beginnings as rough grazing land housing a lean-to farm with a few goats to amuse the high-rise children nearby.

Over a hundred years ago Blanchard Jerrold was writing, "We are drawn to the Kentish Shore, which presents a woeful river-side spectacle. The great ship-yards and lines; the empty sheds, like deserted railway stations; the muddy melancholy bank, and all the evidence of immense doings which are ended, smite us with a sad force . . . this shore, from Woolwich almost to London Bridge, is idle."

Recently Mr. Steatham wrote to me: "Two years ago [1976], I boarded the Russian hydrofoil at Greenwich Pier to take the trip up-stream to Westminster Pier. The speed of that trip amazed me; twelve minutes. But the sight of those once bee-hive wharves and shipping-tiers filled me with so much sadness that I was glad to get off."

And Charlie Jackson echoes thus:

Captain Charlie Jackson.

It's enough to break your heart to see them growing nettles through the wharf-sides now. We thrilled to the sounds of ships – what have the youngsters got now? We've given our heritage to the other European ports; it ain't so long ago I loaded 500 tons of sugar in London, took it to Antwerp, and loaded up again there with self-same sugar packaged to bring back to London at three times the price. You tell me the sense in that, eh? The Dutch is laughing like drains.

Most people have forgotten T. S. Eliot's 'strong brown god' which has fed the capital for centuries, and can just as easily decimate it if the wind is in the right direction. But not all. I travelled down to Greenwich to wait for Don Abel, from Bow, a waterman on his mother's side in a family registered as far back as 1778. He was coming down to pick up three repaired lighters in the tug *Cemenco*,

Captain Don Abel at the wheel of the tug Cemenco.

and we were to take them to Fulham. It was a blustery day, and 'the ditch' still had the ominous choppiness which two weeks before had put central London in such a panic. We travelled past a scene which is largely one of desolation and decay except for the small hopeful sign of new activity here and there such as a modern riverside boatyard for the repair and upkeep of police launches, and Don Abel, watching his young team of lightermen hopping around with all the old agility, set the scene in 1978:

We still register at Watermen's Hall, handling the sweeps is still a vital part of our apprenticeship, and knowledge of the tides. Even with power, there's still a hefty swell round the buttresses of bridges; only last week a small coaster hit the Battersea Bridge and the skipper was killed. Methods may have changed but the river hasn't. Water people no longer live right on the river, but coming downalong I still signal to a friend who lives at the top of that block of flats over there. There are still dead 'uns, but frankly I tend to leave 'em now. The old respect for the river is going; some of the ferry skippers who run up and down with tourists take things too much for granted. I've actually seen 'em reading newspapers whilst carrying fifty to a hundred passengers.

I've an old Dutch barge; she was a roadsman bosun's station for years and I try to teach local kids about the river on it, try to interest the borough schools. We also have a project going along at Wapping with workshops and club-rooms, the idea being to familiarise kids with their own 'high-street', using canoes and boating of all kinds. Lightermen and all sorts give up their weekends to work on it on a voluntary basis . . . there's the old Houses of Parliament.

Actually, my visits had taken me to the Houses of Parliament, known to rivermen as 'the Gasworks' a week or so before to meet Alan Lee Williams, M.P., a man who had worked his time on the river as a lighterman, and the son of a waterman who had plied the treacherous explosives barges in his day. Sadly, dockland is reaching a point very nearly beyond redemption, and in 1974, lightermen, dockies and other riversiders had each contributed one pound to the kitty to inaugurate a campaign entitled 'Transport On Water' from a small disused office at the Royal Albert Docks. Alan Lee Williams was the chairman of this campaign to ensure that national transport policy considered the contribution of our waterways, particularly the River Thames. T.O.W., as a united pressure group has already achieved a great deal, diverting copper, paper and wood-pulp off the roads and on to barges. As recently as the end of January 1979, heavy lorries were prohibited from using Tower Bridge because of the damage they caused to its structure. But their banning only adds more traffic to the already congested roads.

The whole argument of co-ordinating road traffic, rail and river, is a book in itself; suffice to say that we towed two barges containing 300 tons of cement from Fulham to Greenwich in under forty-five minutes. That load, passing quietly and cleanly, disturbed nobody and polluted nothing. By road, the same load would have taken some thirty-eight lorries and Lord knows how much more expense on diesel fuel. The logic of tearing up strips of valuable farming land, communities, and landscape, and disturbing roadside dwellers to the point of suicide when the river lies there empty for all to see, a direct link to the Channel, is lost on me. We should take heed of the likes of Nellie Shackel who, when asked what she would like to say to young Londoners, said:

There's the river under our noses. Every time I cross Battersea Bridge and look at the river empty except for a tug maybe and a few lighters, I burn. There's all those poor people living at Dover with lorries passing their bedroom windows in the middle of the night, and yet in Holland they have 5,000-ton barges taking about 100 lorries off the roads. One day the petrol will be too dear and they'll want the river back and there'll be nobody to teach the youngsters the old skills. Nobody cares, except for a few.

Mrs. Nellie Shackel, daughter of John Taylor of Battersea, the Taylors were lightermen from the early nineteenth century.

In the future, huge catamaran carriers may be used. Known as 'Lash', Lighter aboard ship, they have been described as 'a mother hen laying her eggs'. Such lighters built like containers could take the noise off our roads. We could, like Holland and Germany, carry by water more than seven times the tonnage of road.

The Inland Waterways Association also, is attempting to re-open the network of canals and inland riverways and, hopefully, they and T.O.W. will be able to co-ordinate efforts to revitalise an area where not only is the plant decaying, but redundancies are serious. For dockland itself, a hundred and one schemes come and go with regularity. At the time of writing, a £50,000 feasibility study is being mooted to build an international exhibition centre in dockland, proposals abound for a vast Olympic complex for the 1988 Games, and for a huge dockland city which one hopes will be an improvement on the Barbican.

Could we, however, paradoxically have our cake and eat it as well? Would a greater use of the Thames destroy the efforts of those who have at last coaxed the fastidious salmon back upriver where the water is the cleanest it has ever been for over 300 years? Leslie Wood, Assistant Director for Thames Pollution control, whose aunt's father died in the filthy waters as a passenger on the *Princess Alice*, thinks the two things can exist happily together because the main killer ingredients were sewerage and chemical discharges from riverside plants, and not essentially the shipping itself.

While proposals are made to ensure the Thames has a future as a waterway, it's also encouraging to see that its glorious past is not being forgotten. In the nick of time, organisations like the Maritime Trust, the Society for Spritsail Barge Research, and the Thames Sailing Barge Club have rescued old vessels, and promoted a lively interest in their past history. The East Coast Sail Trust with *Sir Alan Herbert* and *Thalatta* carries thousands of London children on five-day and weekend cruises. *Cambria* at Rochester has been saved by the Maritime Trust, preserving her original cuddy and artifacts of the men who built and sailed her. *Cabby*, the last full size wooden sailing barge built, has been preserved by Crescent Shipping, and pays for herself with promotional trips, as do *May* and *Ethel* for the Tate & Lyle Group. *Ena*, survivor of Dunkirk, and her partner in that adventure, *Pudge*, transport Paul & White's social club members, and the Thames Barge Sailing Club respectively. *Jock* lies waiting for charter at St. Katharine's, her once businesslike hold soft with expensive carpet and glittering drinks bar. *Will Everard*, now called

Inside the cuddy of Will Everard, *a meal of salt junk, suet and jam; the mate 'legs an easy' in his coffin bunk.*

simply *Will*, and *Mirosa* do promotional and charter work for Overseas Containers Limited, and the Blue Circle Group, and many more old sailing barges are lovingly maintained by both enthusiasts and old watermen.

Orinoco, which had sunk in collision, now has a new life at Faversham with a fine new sprit all the way from Canada eighty-three years after her launching at Greenwich. *Victor* was just that, having survived conversion to a motor barge in 1949, motor yacht in 1964, and reappeared in something of her former glory in 1975, victorious again, eighty years since she was first built by Shrubshalls. However, for the most part, they are gone, and I was strangely affected by a photograph of Grandad's *Scud* lying in the mud at Otterham Creek with most of Eastwood's cement barges in the late 40s. *Scud* melted away in the company of *Heron*, *Coot*, *Kappa*, *Gamma*, *Alpha* and *Mid Kent*, her masts and re-sellables stripped, and the worm eating its way in.

However, some of them did not go easily, as Dick Virgo recalled: "My *Sirdar* was a proud lady. When she went to the breakers, she broke herself loose three times. She wasn't ready for the breakers' yard. The third time, we shoved her clean up over the wall at Halstow Creek, but she still slid down in the night and refloated herself. Perhaps she didn't care for her last resting place – it's called Fuston's Bottom. She used to talk to me that one, and complain, by golly!"

Some of the old packhorses have gone, then, and a few are safe, but what of their crews? What of the thousands of people who worked, sweated and strained on them? Where are they now? How

The Sargent brothers in their wherry, Bob Sargent extreme right.

have they survived the demise of sail, and shifting emphases upon the river? Survival takes some odd guises, and Bob Sargent set today's scene, showing how, with an ironic twist of history, the river and show-business have come together once again:

We still handle lighterage, pilots – that sort of thing – though the traffic is a shadow of what it was. We've branched into pleasure cruises too; really, I suppose, back to our beginnings as wherrymen. Our latest venture is *Enchante* which is a fifty-six footer we have on charter for parties. More and more, we get roped in for film companies and television. I've got a commission tomorrow for a T.V. show.

I'll always remember *Cockleshell Heroes*. They asked us to paint up two old police launches to look like German patrol boats for the bit where Trevor Howard is chased by the Jerries. It was a rush job, and we slid them out of our workshop with all the German markings, which gave a few of the locals some nasty turns, I can tell you. Anyway, I'd nailed some dummy rails on them, just for the look of the thing. When they started filming, my heart was in my mouth. All those burly film extras, complete with rifles were leaning on the rails so that the boats were keeling right over, and I was praying they wouldn't fall in. How those screws held I'll never know.

Another film I recall with a laugh involved my brother, too. It was called *Tower of London*. I was on the camera launch, and my brother was lying in the other being filmed. He was concealed on the floor, steering whilst the hero, some big American star, stood up in camera view pre-

tending to steer with his dummy wheel (an old broomstick). Anyway, the shot called for a very narrow miss with us two heading at each other on a collision course. We did it, and well, you wouldn't have liked yer fingers in the gap and when we'd finished the star just dropped in a dead faint; took him about ten minutes to come round.

Dick Virgo still occasionally skippers *Cabby* on her promotional runs, and was himself something of a film star many years before: "1933 I think it was, *Beauty and the Barge* with Margaret Rutherford and Ronald Shiner, but then my dear wife was alive. She went mate for me, and we planned a little place of our own – but she passed away sixteen years ago. Things move on, things change."

Captain and Nanny Fry live in a small community of retired watermen in Greenhithe, once the home of the best coastal sailormen and barge-builders. They tried a fine new house once, but felt totally isolated:

We made a mistake, moved to a really nice house in a cul-de-sac. It was full of young people, and in the day they'd all go out to work so it was quiet, too bloody quiet. So we moved again. We're used to the community feel. You can't be uprooted. That's why I keep in touch, piloting yachts over; I'm not ready to lie down yet. And I still get a shiver going past Dead Man's Island. Most people seem to look on us as old duffers,

Captain and Mrs. Bertie Fry at Greenhythe.

Far left: *Captain Dick Virgo.*

though. I've had a lot to do with restoration of old sailing barges, you know, but it's difficult to make them realise the correct way of doing things on a sailing barge; everything has different names, and so many of the presidents and secretaries are ex-Royal Navy, I've come home sometimes in a right old temper, I can tell you.

Mrs. Fry remembers her early days in London, and sums up what it all means for her now:

There are a lot of us here, all watermen and sailormen and their wives: Mrs. Gammin down the road, Mr. Naylor who was a sail-maker. When I was young, we lived in a road with the Thames at the bottom; it was such a pretty sight to see all the barges tied up waiting for the tide, the sunset behind them; red sails in the sunset, like the song, and behind it, hard work, hard work like it's never known now, but pride; it's an old song, but it meant something to us. We enjoyed ourselves, but we brought three kids up on it and our sons have followed us on to the water. They know if half the country doesn't any more.

Charlie Jackson still lives in Charlton above the deserted grounds where England's 'wooden walls' frothed the waters, and *Harry-Grace-a-Dieu* slipped her 1,500 tons into the reach in 1515. Occasionally he takes the odd charter for Tate & Lyle. "I defy anyone to load a barge under sail now, the know-how is going with us. I cannot sail as a mate or skipper now. Board of Trade stuff – too old they say. But occasionally I go as a cook, or a steward. It ain't the same, down rather than up, but I like still to be on the water."

However, when a sailorman's time came it came, and, sharing something in common with Hamlet, Charlie Jackson was succinct on the subject of his particular falling sparrow.

Except when times was bad, I been on the water all my life. I never did learn to swim. I believed in the lap of the gods. I knew that if we sunk, I'd climb to the top of the mast, and if the water didn't reach the top of my 'ead, I'd survive. If it did reach the top of my head, I wouldn't, simple as that. Naw, I'd ha' sooner gone down gracefully with the old girl. If I had learned to swim – what's the good of it? If I'm thirty miles off shore, what am I going to do? Sink to the bottom and catch a bus 'ome?

APPENDIX

APPENDIX

THE BREAD BASKET
DEPARTMENT

THE SAILORMAN ENJOYED a range of food not granted to the land-locked. It was essentially cheap food, and perhaps nowadays, when our traditional joints of beef and hitherto poor-man's dishes of herring and kipper become delicacies beyond our pocket, some of these old recipes and cooking techniques are worth a second look. The western bargeman's diet was largely a country one, though the London man enjoyed a more varied menu adapting many which he encountered on coastal runs, like the 'Tiddyoggie' Cornish pastie, and if he lived on riverside near the docks, absorbed many international foods imported by foreign sailors, which were adapted by the missus at home – curries, for example, played an important part in a weekly stew of cheap-cuts. Out mudding for days at a time, he might eat largely off the marshes and dykes, and it was some of these little tips which filtered to us on holiday there. Winkle and shrimp gathering I've already mentioned, with, of course, the rule of boiling on a wood fire, and always in (clean) sea-water, and always collected on a falling tide when they were at their freshest. We are becoming inured to the taste of the 'painted lady' which passes as a kipper nowadays, and before not too long, I foresee a time when the beauty of a real smoked bloater or herring will be just a memory. However, any fish can be quite easily smoked, and I have included the technique here for the reader to try.

Time was when the marsh was a walking larder – the grasslands yielding duck, pheasant and wood-pigeons, and the dykes their eels. The ditches (which are distinguished from dykes by being wider and cleaner, and usually with a current), were also a source of food. They still team with minnows which were once trapped by the simple technique of leaving a few bottles submerged overnight to collect, complete with these little fish, in the morning. At one time they were fried in batter, and said to taste not unlike whitebait. Incidentally, why not try fried sprats in batter – if you fry them long enough the bones disintegrate. The secret is to fry them in dripping rather than lard or oil.

Everyone it seems, has now got the mushroom passion. Over a wide expanse of marshland they are difficult at first to pinpoint, but try looking first for the right kind of grass – the areas which appear darker and more lush are liable to attract warm dew, and this is the place to make for. We used to favour the old horse-mushrooms, the dinner-plate variety scorned by the unknowing, and your sense of smell will distinguish a goody from a rogue after a while. However, if in doubt, the old practice was to put them in a bowl of salted water overnight, and those that turned yellow were discarded. They were always fried in bacon fat, and the black ink exuded mopped with bread.

The sea-shore itself was a veritable delicatessen with sea-holly candied for sweetmeats, and sea-kale and badderlocks cooked as a convenient vegetable. Limpets and cockles can be fried once again in batter, and oysters, should you be so lucky, should be eaten the correct way, which was described to me by an old sailor. They should be eaten from the flat part of the shell, not the deep; there should be no 'juice' to an oyster – in fact this is its 'leavings' to put it politely, and it is no wonder that many people are ill from this. The oyster should be 'kissed' with the lips and crushed against the palate with the tongue, not swallowed whole, so there you have it.

Wandering round the fish-shops in central London, I am constantly amazed by the seemingly fastidious housewife who actually pays good money for a mackerel or herring which, to put it mildly, is three parts round the proverbial bend, in the misguided belief that a corpse which hangs limply over the hand is fresh, or discarding the much meatier cock crab for a bigger-shelled female (which has a broader tail flap) in the belief that there's more of a meal under the shell.

The days when riverside marsh families hunted the edible frog and maintained their own cress beds, or called in at Leigh for the fine wine produced there, are way, way past, and indeed many of our meals have spread to become the normal complement of everyone's freezer. However, there is, as in everything, a right way and a wrong way which can make all the difference between a feast and a frizzle, and following are some of the favourite riverside dishes which once typified the waterborne family. The golden rule, however, is to buy them fresh and cook them immediately; the instruction seen in a recent magazine article which ran, 'First open your tin of herrings' is definitely out! The meals are simple fare, and include one or two very familiar standbys, like suet which was as much of a staple to the sailorman as the potato was to the Irishman, and eaten either the Suffolk way, before the main dish, or the T.S.B. way, in meat puddings, savoury form, or fried with bacon as a hefty breakfast. They are familiar, but their method of preparation and ingredients observed on the advice of the very people who should know, make all the difference.

SMOKING YOUR OWN FISH

Any kind will do. Clean and scale. Rub with sea salt – the insides too. Let this stand overnight. Wrap in greaseproof paper then damp newspaper four times the thickness of the fish. Place the parcel in ashes and allow it to smoulder but not burn – 3 lbs. of fish take about 40 minutes. Little ones (sprats) take about 20 minutes. (Boning a fish is easy, if you slit it from head to tail, place it inside down, and press hard, then pull out backbone from tail.)

EELS

You may care to try catching them yourself by one of the age-old methods. Try frying them in dripping after cutting them into 2 in. pieces. The Londoner's way, however (and they must be purchased live), is to jelly them and eat cold:

Put 2 in. pieces into saucepan, and add ½ pint of cold water, adding salt, vinegar, parsley and a bay leaf. Bring to the boil and simmer for 45 minutes. Take out the parsley and bay leaf, and stir in some lemon juice (fresh). Leave to cool for several hours so that the stock forms into a succulent jelly.

RED HERRINGS

Assuming one is making a few for the larder, for 10 herrings: gut and scale them, leaving the heads on. Soak in red vinegar overnight and drain them well. Pack them really tight, preferably in a stone pot, putting layers of sea salt, bay leaves, sugar and black pepper between. Cover the herrings and weight them until the salt turns 'briny', ensuring that they are always submerged. Store in a cool place, ideally on marble. Before eating them, some prefer to soak them, the time depending on how long they've been in the brine. It's a matter of taste.

ALTERNATIVE METHOD

Cover the herrings with boiling water and leave for a while, then drain. Soak in milk for 1 hour, then cut into pieces, and dress with vinegar (and oil if fancied). Garnish with chopped gherkins and diced boiled potatoes, dressing it all with oil and red vinegar.

MUSSEL AND BACON SKEWERS

(All the dishes are best done on a wood or charcoal fire to absorb the smoke taste, but this makes an unusual barbecue dish, eaten with hunks of bread or rice.) Dice salt bacon pieces, and open mussels. Thread on to skewer – bacon at both ends, and suspend over heat, allowing the bacon fat to baste them. Take off occasionally, and roll the skewer in breadcrumbs and accumulated juices. Sprinkle with black pepper, and if you have it, occasionally dip in cream whilst eating. (Scallops or limpets taste just as good, and if you do not want to thread mussels on a skewer, put them in juices to fry under the suspended bacon – though they don't absorb the wood-smoke taste so well.)

QUORN OR SALT JUNK (BACON)

Salted pork or bacon was a staple dish, and whilst we cannot imitate the steady motion of the vessel which kept the brine moving as it cooked, we can ensure a good taste by boiling it always in sea salt, slowly, and for a long time. To add a spicy taste, drop in a little of the faithful old Esil or vinegar, or, for a sweet taste, a spoonful of honey. Try and buy a piece direct from the carcass, rather than the dyed remnant with all its juices stunted in plastic.

QUORN ROLL

Roll out suet into a crust to about ¼ in. thick. Lay on it ¾ in. strips of quorn, sprinkle with sage, onion pieces, and roll the lot tightly into a piece of floured white cotton. Tie off ends and place in boiling water, boiling slowly for 2 hours. Unwrap on to a hot dish, sprinkle with parsley, and surround with fried diced potato and fried carrots. Serve with thick brown gravy.

SEA CHOWDER
(To make about 2 quarts)

6–8 pieces of flounder, herring or cod	¼ cup flour
¼ lb. diced, salt junk	2 cups milk
2 onions (diced)	teaspoon sugar, sea salt, black pepper
2 large potatoes (diced)	dash of thyme, cayenne, rosemary
2 tablespoons butter	½ cup of yoghurt or cream

Place fish in an iron skillet or heavy pan, cover with water enough only to submerge them and boil for 15 minutes till fish flakes. Remove fish, and preserve stock. Add diced junk and cook over low heat till browned. Add onion till soft, then fish stock and potatoes with a little water to cover only. Cook for 20 minutes until tender but not mushy. Melt butter in saucepan and add flour, stirring till bubbly. Stir in milk slowly till sauce is thick. Add seasonings. Blend in cream and add to the vegetable mixture. Add cooked fish. Leave in cool place to blend flavours. Heat to serve, adding a knob of butter, and parsley – some also like a pinch of curry powder or paprika.

PUPTON PIGEONS

The once popular idea of eating month-old pigeons or 'squabs' seems a bit heartless, but the upriver lighterman once made a practice of netting them, and here is one dish for young pigeons which can still be purchased at some butchers: this would feed 2.

2 young pigeons
¾ lb. pastry made with dripping and butter
sea salt, pepper, a dusting of flour
brown gravy, with or without cider or beer

Season flour, and rub the pigeons. Roll out pastry to about ⅛ in. Divide it and wrap each bird, sealing pastry by moistening the edges. Tie each into cotton rag very tightly. Place in boiling water and boil for approx. 1½ hours. Unwrap and slide on to dish, pour on gravy. Eat straight away – the pastry imparts a marvellous flavour.

SCALLOP & MUSHROOM PIE

1 lb. scallops
¾ cup milk
¼ teaspoon sea salt
3 tablespoons butter or
  margarine
¼ lb. large sliced mushrooms

2 tablespoons flour
¼ cup of sherry or ale
2 cups hot, freshly mashed
  potato (seasoned with herbs)
chopped parsley

In a small saucepan combine scallops, milk and salt. Bring to boil, reducing heat, and simmer for 5 minutes. Drain, reserving the juice. Melt butter in pan. Remove from heat, and add mushrooms, return to brown for a few minutes. Blend in the flour, and stir in reserved milk. Bring to boil, stirring all the time, till it thickens, then reduce heat and simmer for 5 minutes. Add all the scallops to the sauce, stir in sherry or other liquor (optional), return to boil. Pour into a pie plate. Spoon mashed potato on top, sprinkle with slivers of butter and pepper, grill till browned. Serve immediately with chopped parsley on top. (Makes 4.)

WATER SOUCHY (A Greenwich favourite from the Dutch *Sootje*)
(Originally a way of utilising odd small fish caught in the nets, an
absolute must before fried whitebait.) Try buying a small quantity of
scraps – add sprats, squid – any type of cheap fish.
1 lb. assorted fish – whitebait, sprats, squid etc.
a bouquet of tied herbs – parsley, rosemary
1 lemon, sea salt and peppercorns
(If the parsley has its roots, all the better.)
Put plenty of water into a saucepan, and put in assorted fish. Add sea
salt and pepper (about ½ oz, to every quart of water). Chop up all
the parsley (fresh horseradish which grows wild all over Kent will
make a hot variant, though use ¼ as much). Add this to the mixture,
and simmer for about 1 hour. Strain, and keep your juice, popping
any nice pieces of fish still evident into it. Add the sliced lemon. The
soup should be a nice green colour and clear. Drink from mugs with
fingers of toast, or fried bread.

LONDON DOUBLE PIE

2 lbs. fresh minced meat (best
  to mince yourself)
4 oz. sliced onions
4 oz. mushrooms – the bigger
  ones, not button
2 oz. dripping from roast or
  lamb
curry powder to taste

1 oz. flour
¾ pint good stock or gravy
1 egg (new laid if possible)
1 lb. savoury pastry (shortcrust)
sea salt and milled pepper to
  taste

Set oven at 425F° or Gas 7. Fry meat and onions in dripping for 5
minutes, add mushrooms, stir in curry powder, and 1 oz. flour.
Cook for further 2–3 minutes. Add stock and seasoning, bring to
boil and simmer for 15 minutes. Line a 2-pint pie dish with ⅔ of the
pastry, put in filling, cover with remaining pastry and brush with
beaten egg. Bake till pastry is golden (approx. 20 minutes), reduce
temperature to 350F° or Gas 4 and bake for further 20–25 minutes.
Serve with mashed potatoes, mashed or marrowfat peas.

POT BEANS

1 lb. haricot beans (having been soaked overnight)

¼ lb. diced bacon junk (the fattier the better)

2 tablespoons black treacle

diced onion or small whole ones

teaspoon mustard and curry powder (cider optional)

sea salt and black pepper

Boil the beans for about 4–5 minutes. Strain into the stone-pot together with all the other ingredients. Fill the pot with water to cover. Cover tightly, and preferably leave on a stove overnight to cook slowly, or if you are doing something else which requires a long slow oven at 250F° or Gas ½, leave for 4 hours. Delicious cold or hot (serves 5–6).

KENTISH HUFFKINS

½ oz. fresh yeast (or 1½ teaspoons dried)

½ pint warm milk and water

1 lb. white flour

1 oz. lard

½ teaspoon salt

1 teaspoon caster sugar

Make the dough by kneading as ordinary method for plain white bread. Divide the dough after it has risen into 10 equal shares, and shape in flat oval cakes about ½ in. thick. Place well apart on a tray, and push a floured finger into each centre. Cover with a cloth and 'prove' them till they are twice the size. Bake in oven at 450F° or Gas 8 for 15–20 minutes (near the top). Serve hot at their best with salted dripping or butter.

PUDDINGS

'Waste not, want not', was certainly an employed maxim on river-side, and here are some handy ways with left-over bread, plus of course, the mainstay, suet, and its variations.

GASH DOUGHNUTS

If a whole loaf has gone stale on you, cut off the crust, cut the remaining interior into ½ in. thick by 2 in. squares, and deep fry in dripping till golden brown. Toss them in a plate of icing-sugar, and eat straightaway.

JIB SHEET FRITTERS

Cut bread in the same way, this time with the crust. Beat an egg or eggs (say 1 for each 4–5 pieces). Add milk (1 cup for each 4 pieces). Soak bread in this mixture till it is absorbed but not sloppy. Fry in lard or refined dripping till crisp. Serve hot with jam.

HALF–PAY PUDDING

4 oz. suet	8 oz. half currants, half raisins
4 oz. flour	½ pint milk
4 oz. breadcrumbs	2 tablespoons treacle

Mix well, and boil in a mould for about 4 hours.

APPLE BREAD (UTILISING WINDFALLS)

Make bread in the usual way, but with ⅓ less mixture. Make up the mixture, with warm, pulped apples. Then put the mixture into a bread tin and leave it covered to rise by a warm stove or radiator all day (minimum of 8 hours), then bake in the normal way. Eat hot with a sprinkling of caraway seeds.

PLAIN SUET MIXTURE
SUET PUDDING

The following is the basic mixture, but this was eaten under a dozen guises: rolled with jam it was 'Roly Poly', impregnated with dates it was 'Spotty Dick' or 'Spotty Dog', rolled in a ball to fill out stews, it was a dumpling, and fried, it was a substitute for bread on long journeys when the baker could not call.

12 oz plain flour
¼ teaspoon salt
heaped teaspoon baking-
   powder
4–6 oz. chopped suet
enough water to enable
   mixing

Sift the flour, salt and baking powder. Mix in the suet. Add cold water and knead to a dough. Shape into a roll. Put in floured cloth and roll loosely. Tie ends off with string and put in a saucepan of boiling water for 1½–2 hours, topping up now and again. Keep covered. (Serves 6.)

This basic recipe can be mixed with yeast and rolled into balls, after it has been kneaded for some minutes. Then when risen, it is quickly dropped in boiling water for 6–7 minutes, drained, and eaten with jam or treacle as 'Norfolk dumplings'. Again, it can be filled with raw giblets and boiled in a copy of the Chinese 'pau' so favoured by Oriental seamen and passed on to docksiders. Or it can be filled with raw steak and kidney, and boiled in the Londoners' 'steak and kidney pud', though as Charlie Jackson and Dick Virgo insisted, the meat must go in raw, not cooked. Spotted dick is also delicious cold with a spot of butter, and sliced like bread. Though the essential in all suet boils is the use of the boiling cloth and tape or string, a lot of modern recipes suggest greaseproof, or, Lord help us, plastic film, but the old-timers swear by their old rags – and indeed, the same one was boiled and re-used over and over.

BIBLIOGRAPHY

Benham, Hervey, *Once Upon a Tide*, Harrap, 1955

Carr, Frank G. G., *Sailing Barges*, Peter Davies, 1931 and 1951

Doré, Gustave, and Blanchard Jerrold, *London – A Pilgrimage*, 1872

Harris, Harry Thomas, *Under Oars*, Stepney Book Publications and Centerprise

London, Jack, *Into The Abyss*, 1902

March, Edgar, J., *Spritsail Barges of Thames and Medway*, David and Charles

Mayhew, Henry, *London Life and London Poor*

Mee, Arthur, *North London*, Hodder and Stoughton, 1972

Mitchell, R. J., and M. D. R. Leys, *A History of London Life*, Pelican, 1958

Williams, Harry, *South London*, Robert Hale, 1949

Wood, Walter, *Survivors' Tales of Famous Shipwrecks*, E. P. Publishing, Ltd., 1974

Fishing Boats and Barges, John Lane, 1922

PICTURE SOURCES

The author and publisher are indebted to the following picture libraries for certain illustrations in this book:

Alan Cordell Collection, page 108; British Museum, page 28; Cowes Maritime Museum, page 146; *Daily Telegraph*, page 184; Greenwich Local History Library, pages 34, 46, 50, 102 and 112; Imperial War Museum, pages 130 and 174; London and Rochester Trading Company, page 190; Maritime Trust, page 86; Mary Evans Picture Library, pages 30, 74, 100, 101; Museum of London, page 58; National Maritime Museum, page 27; *Punch*, page 139; Radio Times Hulton Picture Library, pages 71, 73, 90, 94, 135, 150, 182, 188 and facing the title page; Southwark Library and Museum Services, pages 82, 111 and 132; Syndication International Ltd., page 122.